No part of this publication may be reproduced in any form, stored in a retrieval system, or transmitted, in any form, or by any means – electronic, mechanical, photocopying, recording, or otherwise, without the prior written permission of the author, except in brief quotations within critical articles and reviews

The Alzheimer's Roller Coaster
The Story Of Our Ride

Copyright © 2013 Carolyn Mers

All rights reserved.

ISBN: 1484088964
ISBN 13: 978-1484088968

Pat,
May God Bless
you on your roller
coaster ride in life! Aug. 2013
Carolyn

THE
ALZHEIMER'S
ROLLER COASTER

THE STORY OF OUR RIDE

CAROLYN MERS

ACKNOWLEDGEMENTS

While I have had a great number of family and friends encouraging me to turn my journal writings into a book that could possibly be of benefit to other caregivers and care partners in their own Alzheimer's journey, this book would never have been written without the extra push from friend, author, and modern day pen-pal, (aka – email) Curtiss Ann Matlock. Thank you, my mentor, from the very depths of my heart for convincing me that I could do this. I will be eternally grateful for your endless support in this project. Much love and many blessings to you and yours.

Roller coaster cover photo taken near Seattle, WA by Teal Weichman of Rainbows'n'Frogs Photography, Houston, TX. Thank You, it is a perfect shot.

To the O'Fallon Illinois Writers Guild, for taking me under your wing; sharing your knowledge of writing and publishing tips made this endeavor become a reality. Thanks to each and every one of you.

To the very generous friends and colleagues who took the time to edit the manuscript; you helped bring this book to life.

I could not have gotten through this entire ordeal without the love and constant help from my wonderful husband, Dan. Thank you for always being by my side, for being my rock. Your support through this has been amazing. I love you more than you can possibly know!

To my daughters, I hope you do not have to go through the same hell that I have been going through. I hope by writing this journal, that you will have a better understanding of what this disease can do to everyone touched by the uncertainty and the complex paths that you end up going down. I hope you will have a better knowledge and understanding of what is needed for your own sake as well as mine. Do not be afraid to seek help. If you allow God to be your guide, you will find the answers that you need.

But above all else, I thank God for giving me the strength to carry on this entire mission, for giving me the words needed to tell my story. I know He is with me always. I appreciate all the angels He has provided to me and for their help all along the way, especially the ones who were not aware that they too were on a mission from above!

Thank you to each and every one of you for your help and support.
GOD BLESS ALL OF YOU!!

This book is dedicated to my mother
Virginia Mae (Wayne) Manring

To the wonderful life we have shared, to this crazy, wild and often unexplainable ride that we are now taking. May our story somehow help others to understand and cope with their own journey through this world called Alzheimer's /dementia.

TABLE OF CONTENTS

ACKNOWLEDGEMENTS

DEDICATION

A MOTHER'S WISH

THE SCARIEST ROLLER COASTER RIDE OF MY LIFE

WHAT IS THIS THING CALLED ALZHEIMER'S

MY PERSONAL CHECKLIST

PREFACE

1	MOM'S STORY	26
2	THE BEGINNING SIGNS	30
3	OUR MOVE BACK TO ILLINOIS	36
4	THE RIDE IS PICKING UP SPEED	56
5	THE EVENTS OF 2008	61
6	THE EVENTS OF 2009	78
7	THE MOVE TO ASSISTED LIVING	127
8	THE EVENTS OF 2010	135
9	THE EVENTS OF 2011	150
10	MOVE TO THE MEMORY CARE UNIT	160
11	GRANDMA'S QUILT	168

12	PLASTIC PINWHEELS	179
13	ONE YEAR LATER	185
14	SHE'S A STUPID WOMAN	192
15	CAUTION! SHARP TURN AHEAD!	196
16	THE RIDE GOES ON	202
17	CONCLUSION	209
18	A LETTER FROM LINDA	214
19	AN OPEN LETTER TO MY DAUGHTERS	218

I found the following letter in the newspaper early on in our Alzheimer's ride, (most likely a Dear Abby column, but I am not sure), I print it here because I believe they are the same words that my Mother would say to me, if she were able:

A MOTHER'S WISH

If ever that day comes in my life when I become old and senile, be gentle with me. When I can't remember and can't do for myself, help me. Help me to remember those days of your youth. Help me to laugh, and laugh with me. When one day I don't remember you, know, that I don't wish it to be that way. Don't give up on me.

Help keep me neat and pretty. Help me to keep my self - respect. Don't laugh at me for things I do, that you don't understand. Keep me company. Just let me know that you care. And finally, when that time comes for me to go home to my beloved Savior, don't be sad for me.......for, I will be whole and complete again, and one day we will meet again in Paradise.

Your Loving Mother

Author Unknown

THE SCARIEST ROLLER COASTER
RIDE OF MY LIFE

For most people the word "roller coaster" conjures up thoughts and memories of fun and exciting times. They envision, loud pulsating, energizing music, friends laughing and screaming with excitement, arms up in the air, the wind blowing through their hair. I myself have never enjoyed roller coaster rides, I have always been afraid of the dark tunnels, the unexpected dips and sharp unexpected turns; the banks that make you feel like you would fall out of the car. The slow chugging climb up the steep hills always filled me with the impending doom of free falling to the bottom, wondering when the safety of having my feet firmly on the ground again would ever happen. Would I live through it, or would my heart just suddenly stop from the fear of the unknown?

Most of my family knows how I feel about roller coasters, and yet on occasion I have been talked into riding them. A good example would be in 2008, we took our Grandson, Kane to DisneyWorld, where he talked me into riding the Rock & Roll Roller Coaster. He had already ridden it a couple of times and assured me that it wasn't that bad. When that torturous ride finally ended I could not get out of the car fast enough. I know that both of my feet were not even squarely on the platform when I was already turned around and yelling at him, "DO NOT EVER ASK ME TO RIDE A ROLLER COASTER AGAIN!!!" I still feel very bad about the way I yelled at him, and I can still see the terror in his eyes, afraid of his Granny who had just turned into a screaming wild woman, (but honestly, never believe a 13 year old boy who says, "It isn't that bad, Granny, you can do it!") I thought I was going to die on that ride. I wish I hadn't yelled so harshly at him, but I was truly terrified! And now with both of my feet planted firmly on solid ground, I am on the scariest roller coaster ride ever.

Nothing has prepared me for the roller coaster ride that I am on now. This roller coaster is called, Alzheimer's disease, or Dementia. We have been riding this roller coaster for well over 10 years now. This scary ride seems to go on and on, I don't know how long it will last or where it will take me. Some days we coast along on a smooth track, at a comfortable pace, but I certainly do not know when the next uphill climb or sudden drop will take place.

Today, these hills and valleys, turns, banks and loops consist of doctors, lawyers, creditors, Medicare &

Medicaid caseworkers and all of their paperwork and bureaucracy. The dark tunnels are the dark untouchable areas of Mom's memory. The place where her life is tucked away and out of touch to the rest of us standing by, waiting and watching and feeling helpless, a place that she is no longer able to share with us. Having never dealt with any of these issues before, I am totally riding on a new track and I do not know where I am going. I do not even know how to plan for the unexpected turns and twists. Then there are the issues of family members, caring, but not connected. They pop in and out like the scary holograms jumping in front of your face, just enough to let you know they are there, but not tangible enough to be of any genuine help or support. Some, asking endless repetitive questions, others, asking nothing at all, some, having no opinion about any of the issues.

I don't know a lot about Mom's younger years, but I do know that she did enjoy roller coasters, but this is one ride she didn't ask for, (nor did I). We did not purchase a ticket for this ride, but because of my love for the woman who gave me life, the woman who stood by me when I was a child, with my skinned knees, bumps and bruises, who stood by me when I was going through rough times in my own adult life, I am here to be her friend on this ride that she is taking. Mom may not know that she needs me to be there, she may not understand exactly what is going on with her life, she may even resent my interference, but I am here to see that she safely makes it to the end of the ride. So with my seatbelt buckled, arms up in the air and wanting to scream (at any number of people, for a lot of different reasons), here I am on the scariest roller coaster ride of my life, for as long as the ride lasts.

> Only God the "Ride Operator" knows
> the length and course of this ride.
> I wonder, if there will be cotton candy
> when it's over?

While my ride is far from over, I want to let you know up front, that in the beginning, while there were many dark days, filled with confusion and turmoil, for both of us, we are currently in a calm state. Once we both learned to accept what was happening to **US**, we both found ourselves in a better place. I don't really know if Mom "knows" she has dementia, but I do know that she is currently in a relaxed, content space. Today, I know that when I go to visit her, she allows me to visit her, in her world. In her world we talk about what is important to her, not me. We usually talk about Elvis Presley, her cousin, Sheriff Mearl Justus, her special friend Richard, or my brother Jim; all whom she believes visit her often. These people are important in her world, so that makes them important in my world too.

I have come to realize that in the beginning when visits were the hardest, it was because I still wanted Mom to be a part of my life, as we had once known it. I wanted her to be involved with me and talk about what used to be important to both of us. I wanted her to care about what I was doing and what was going on in my life, like she used to. I wanted our conversations to be "conversations," a give and take, a sharing of thoughts. I wanted her to somehow understand that she was not being reasonable and rational in her thinking. Once I realized that this ride wasn't about me, and I learned to just be content to be in her world for a few hours each day, my life got easier. I have learned that when I visit in her world, I am at peace and am comforted by the telling of her stories (no matter how far-fetched they may be, they are real to her.) I have learned how to look for the joy in each visit, h earing her laugh and watching her smile brings me joy. Sometimes we create special simple memories together, even though I know she won't remember the memories that we are creating...... I will!

While Mom is not able to communicate with me like we did in the past, we have now developed our own way of communicating. She may not always know who I am, she may not want to kiss me or allow me to kiss her, but we always put our foreheads together, and look each other in the eyes. She tells me to be careful, I tell her to be good, and with a little devilish smile on her face she replies, "That's no fun, but I'll try!"

**MOTHER'S DAY 2004
SHRINE OF OUR LADY OF THE SNOWS**

WHAT IS THIS THING CALLED ALZHEIMER'S?

As with any disease, the research is always on-going. What is reported today will most likely be changed next week. What we knew yesterday is no longer true. At first it seemed that everything I read directly pointed to the fact that this disease is hereditary. Which is very scary for someone in my position, am I doomed to follow in my Mother's footsteps?

Now in just a few short years the documentation is proving not only that this disease is gradually taking hold of our minds years before we or anyone else is aware of, but we may have some control over our destiny.

We all know that we need to be exercising to maintain a healthy body *(yes, I know, I need to move more, but I just can't seem to find the time to actually do it. I am very good at procrastinating, but that is not a true statement either. The true fact is that I am overloaded with commitments. I am multi-tasking to the 10th degree, barely a free moment in any given day.)* The doctor, who 5 years ago, I had never met, but I had made up my mind that I did not care for him or his methods of taking care of my Mother, was now becoming the person that I leaned on. He is not only my Mother's physician, but I feel that every visit is a pep talk for me, for my own sake. His words of exercising, both the body and the mind, are meant for me, more so than his actual patient, my Mother. He knows, she is not exercising, or doing the word puzzle books that he had told her several years ago that she should be doing. *(He can also tell just by looking at me that I am not exercising either!)*

Some of the newest reports are stressing that what is good for our body is also very good for our brains. We need to reduce the refined sugars and starches, concentrate on fresh natural fruits and vegetables. Drink lots of water to keep the brain hydrated. *(Sounds a LOT like what I have been hearing for years at my numerous attempts at Weight Watchers and a hundred other diet plans!)*

Recent studies have also shown that people who smoke in their early formative years and into their thirties are more likely to develop Alzheimer's. This makes so much sense to me, since we know that smoking restricts blood vessels, it would certainly include the blood vessels in the brain. Yes, Mom was a heavy smoker for probably 30-40 years. As long as I can remember Mom was a smoker until just a few years ago, when she quit cold turkey. Also, high cholesterol levels at an early age should be monitored. (High cholesterol runs in her family.) The effects of high cholesterol are more destructive than just a group of numbers that doctor's try to warn us to control. For most of us, those cholesterol numbers do not have a "*real*" meaning. We don't "*feel*" sick, nor do we "*feel better*" if we have it under control. But now, there is even more reason to want to pay attention to those numbers.

There was one report that I read that linked Zinc to Alzheimer's. Zinc is in so many products, but for me, most notably in denture creams and fixatives. Mom has worn dentures and used the same fixative for as long as I can remember. Low and behold, I've noticed that those boxes now say, "Does not contain Zinc." (*I have to wonder why they removed the Zinc.*)

I have also read somewhere, and I have to admit….I do not know where I read it, so I cannot vouch for its validity. But it said that sex is good for the brain. The endorphins released during orgasm help to keep the brain stimulated and healthy. So, good sex = good brain??? Hmmm!!!! Interesting!!! I wonder, since women live longer than men, and most do not engage in any sexual activity after losing a spouse, could this be another factor of why there are more women than men sitting in nursing homes? This could be a theory worth investigating.

I have developed my own personal checklist of what I can do for myself and my kids. This checklist may or may not ward off any hereditary genes, but it can give me a tool for doing what I can to help myself to lessen the risks of this terrible disease. It can also be a tool to maintain dialogue with my girls. I want to tell them stories about my life, about their lives, I want them to be spared some of the drama that I have stumbled through during the past 10 years.

MY PERSONAL CHECKLIST

- Try to take control of my diet and exercise routines.

- Make the effort to play a variety of games and puzzles.

- Learn a new art or foreign language.

- Read more. (This includes fiction as well as research material).

- Start a journal now, of my own childhood memories and stories to share with my children and grandchildren.

- Be sure that my children know and have access to our insurance and financial matters.

- Appoint a Power of Attorney

- Admit and discuss with the girls, the possibilities and effects of Alzheimer's, and what my wishes are.

- Mentally prepare for the move that will one day lead Dan and me to senior living.

- Spend time laughing with friends.

- Enjoy life and all that it has to offer.

PREFACE

Before I get into my story, I want to say that this is about my ride with my Mother, my thoughts and fears, how this ride has affected the two of us, from my perspective. It is not intended to promote any medical facts or findings, nor is it intended to dispel any myths. I apologize up front if I have hurt anyone's feelings, or have overlooked how anyone else may have perceived an incident, but it is the way circumstances were observed by me at the moment, this is the telling of my story.

While I felt that this was a story that needed to be shared with others, it was also quite difficult to open up my heart to the world. It took more strength than I could ever have imagined, to actually follow through, and let the whole outside universe into "our world."

You will find that the book at times, is direct diary outtakes from my personal journal, with thoughts and feelings interjected. At other times it is the telling of stories, past and present; sometimes happy, sometimes sad. You will find that at various times and without warning, we jump from the present to the past, and back again. It has no real beginning, nor end.

Welcome to the world of Alzheimer's disease

Welcome to "The Alzheimer's Roller Coaster"

1

MOM'S STORY

My Mother, Virginia Mae (Wayne) Manring, was born April 18, 1929, in Chicago Illinois to John William Wayne and Mae Viola (Jerome) Wayne.

What I know about her young life is very sketchy. She never talked much of her youth, teen years, or even her married life. As I have come to realize, she was very much like her Mother, Mae Wayne. Grandma never talked about her life either. She was a very, very private person. Which is quite sad, because I think, for a woman who lived for a very healthy 95 years, she probably had an interesting life and could have shared some wonderful stories, shared some memories, as well as history. Whenever she was directly asked about the past, her reply was, "that was in the past, no need to talk about it." And that was pretty much my Mom's philosophy too.

I don't remember hearing very many life stories, only how wonderful it was in Chicago, despite growing up poor, and not having a bedroom to sleep in. The only doll she ever owned came from a neighbor lady who felt sorry for her one Christmas when she didn't have a new doll to play with, like the other little girls in the building. She treasured that little porcelain baby doll her whole life. I now have it tucked away in a safe place.

Growing up on the south side of Chicago, I do know that she was well aware of Al Capone and other mobsters who ruled the city. Al Capone had even tried to rent a room in the building where she lived.

Frank Sinatra was an up and coming singer when Mom saw him in person. She said that in those days you could go and pay for a show, and stay for the next one too. Which she and her friends did. She always told stories of how Frank would have to tell people to please not sing the songs with him, because they had already seen the show. There were other people in the audience, seeing the show for the first time, and they deserved to hear him sing it, as it had been intended.

She attended dances with her first true love, Richard. They danced to the big band sounds of Wayne Greg, Ozzie Nelson and Glenn Miller. She talked of going to the museums for free and the ball games for a dime. Dates were usually spent at the dime store, hanging out with friends at the soda fountain.

Mom's favorite two movies were, "Gone with the Wind," and "The Wizard of Oz". On opening day of "The Wizard of Oz," several of the real Munchkins were there to greet the people as they arrived to see the movie. Later, whenever the movie was on TV, she always pointed out the munchkins that she had met. When she saw the opening of "Gone with the Wind," she and her girlfriends sat through two back-to-back showings of the movie. I can't imagine sitting there that long! But she knew the movie word for word.

When she wanted to attend Mercy High School in Chicago and her parents could not afford the tuition and the uniforms, she set out to put herself through high school. Even though she was underage, she lied about her age and managed to get a job and paid all of her own expenses throughout high school. She did this without resentment or ridicule of her parent's financial means. Instead she held her head up high and was proud of what she had achieved on her own. When her Dad attended her graduation, he told her just how proud he was of her accomplishments, and that it was a beautiful school and he understood why she had wanted to attend Mercy High School.

Shortly after graduation the family moved back to Cahokia, and she had to leave Richard behind. (*I later learned that she never forgot her first love, and he is very important in her "new" world).*

But real stories of her life and dreams, what she liked or disliked about school, there was nothing that I can relate to, or fantasize about. However, in very recent years out of the blue she would start to tell a story, and if I asked why I had never heard this before, her answer would always be, "it never came up before." This is doubly sad because, now at this early stage of her disease, I wish I knew some of her stories, so that I could share with her the things from her past. I wish I could remind her of some of her happy memories. I wish I could reach some part of those dark tunnels in her mind that would make her smile. Now when she tells her stories, I have to wonder what is true, what is fantasy? How is one to know? How do we sort fact from fiction and does it really matter now?

2

THE BEGINNING SIGNS

It is very easy to overlook the beginning signs of Dementia simply as the normal aging process. Learning and accepting the fact that what you are witnessing is more serious is a very difficult idea to wrap your head around, especially if no one else has the same thoughts as you do, but somewhere deep down in your own heart you know it is true.

In the year 2000, Dan and I were living in Houston, TX and becoming quite homesick, in large part due to both of our aging Mothers, and feeling the need to be closer to them. We were hoping to get transferred back to St. Louis, but ended up in Kenosha, WI instead. While it wasn't exactly home, the 6 hour drive from Kenosha was a whole lot closer to Fairview Heights, IL, than the 18 hour drive from Houston.

Mom still worked full time as a seamstress for Bridal Originals, as a seamstress making formals and wedding gowns. My brother Jim still lived at home with Mom. He never married and did not have any children. He did have a girlfriend who lived on the far south outskirts of St. Louis. He would go to her house on the weekends, leaving Mom the responsibility of caring for his menagerie of several fish tanks, parrot, and gerbil. Besides caring for Jim's zoo, Mom's weekends were filled with doing all of their laundry, grocery shopping, house cleaning, and weeding the flower beds. Jim's responsibilities involved keeping the grass mowed and her car clean.

Mom and I spent a lot time talking on the phone, even though she was lonely with him gone the entire weekend, she would never complain about it, because at last, he had a girlfriend, and she would never deny him that, or anything else that he wanted to do. She never had, and she wasn't going to start now. Her life was centered on making sure that he was happy and content, no matter what sacrifices that meant for herself.

Through our many phone calls, I began to notice that her thought process was slowing down somewhat, and I also noticed that she would repeat conversations that we had talked about on previous phone calls. At first, I wrote it off as she didn't remember telling me that particular story, because she had probably told one of my aunts, or to my sister, and not me. But it kept happening more and more.

There was a missed step in a restaurant that led to having to wear a cast for 8 weeks, and then a purse left behind at another restaurant, and then the phone calls started, asking how to make things such as egg salad and tuna salad. She never once said she forgot how to make those things, she always said it had been so long since she made them, that she wasn't exactly sure what went in. Jim didn't like them; so therefore, she didn't make them very often. With him gone for the weekend, it would be a nice treat to have.

It was Christmas 2001, Dan and I had driven down from Kenosha and we were all going to go to my sister Linda's house in Effingham, IL for Christmas Eve dinner. Christmas at Linda's meant a house full of laughter and lots of conversation among her husband, their five grown children, their spouses and numerous grandchildren of all ages.

Mom and I were in her kitchen preparing food to take to Linda's house. Mom was making deviled eggs, she had the eggs peeled and cut in half, she added the Miracle Whip, mustard, salt and pepper. She went to the refrigerator and grabbed the jar of pickle relish and started dumping it in. I was quite surprised, I asked, "When did you start putting pickle relish in your deviled eggs?" Her eyes glazed over and became stone cold; she slammed the jar down on the table and said, "I HAVE **ALWAYS** PUT RELISH IN MY DEVILED EGGS!!" *(Now maybe some people do add relish, but we never have).*

I was dumbfounded and tried to control my voice, and said, "I know it has been a long time since I have had your deviled eggs, I guess I have forgotten that you do that." She just glared at me and continued to dump relish in, as she replied with, **"Well, I guess you did forget, because I have always made it this way!"** She finished up her eggs, put them in the Tupperware container, and put it in the fridge. I finished up my dish, and we got ready to go. We all piled in the car for the hour drive to my sisters. When we arrived at Linda's house and were walking across the yard to go in, Mom says, "Oh, I forgot my eggs." I turned around to head back to the car, when she said, "No, at home, I forgot to bring them." I chuckled and shook my head. Inside the house, I pulled Linda aside and asked her about the relish in deviled eggs, and she said that she had never had them with relish either. So I knew it wasn't me who had forgotten how Mom had made her deviled eggs.

On another night during that same holiday visit, we had dinner at home and then decided to go see a movie. When we returned home, there was a strong gas odor when we walked in the door. Dan went straight to the stove and saw that a burner had been left on, no flame, just enough for the gas to be released. He went around opening windows and doors. I grabbed Jim by the arm and pulled him outside and asked if this had happened before; and he confirmed that this was not the first time, but that he did not know what to do about it. I questioned how he could go off to his girlfriends' house for long weekends and leave Mom alone knowing this. I asked why he never said anything about it. I got his usual reply of a shrug of his shoulders.

On our drive back to Kenosha, Dan and I vowed that we would try to make more frequent trips back to check on things and that I would most certainly be making a lot more phone calls, as well as quick trips back to visit and see things for myself. Somehow, we would have to figure out a way to move back home sooner, rather than later.

With my sister living an hour away and all other aunts and uncles living even further, it was hard to find someone who could truly keep tabs on things. While I would have thought about hiring someone to check on the situation, no one else thought it was that bad. Just simply aging and she was OK; I was making too much out of it.

My advice to anyone having these same doubts is to go with your gut instinct. Let others call you a worry wart if they want to; you really do know in your heart what it is and it is best to be proactive, seek doctors who are willing to listen to you and then get second opinions, rather than regret what may happen if you don't. My fear of upsetting Mom and making her mad made me react slower than what I really felt I should. If I had insisted that everyone talk about the issues, then quite possibly we could have slowed down the declining process, or at the very least, we could have handled the situation very differently. We could have had open honest discussions; we could have handled things together. I was put in the very difficult position of seeing what was happening to my Mom and not being able to help her see and understand what was happening, while also trying to preserve her dignity. While never being easy, The Alzheimer's Roller Coaster could have been a little bit smoother ride, if everyone could have just talked.

3

OUR MOVE BACK TO ILLINOIS

Circumstances with Dan's job prompted him to decide that he was ready to take an early retirement and we started to lay the groundwork for moving back home. We knew that this decision did not mean sitting on a porch in a rocking chair. We knew it would be hard work to turn the ceramic shop into a full functioning business making more money than just a few dollars of fun money. We also knew that there was the very real likelihood that Dan would take on some consulting positions with his IT background.

We looked for land where we could build a business and a home. We looked at homes that a small business could be operated from. We looked as far south as Dupo and as far northeast as Effingham; nothing seemed to be the right fit for one reason or another.

February of 2003, I found a house. It may not have been the house of our dreams, but it was convenient to Mom, it was convenient enough to get to Elaine (Dan's Mom in Columbia, IL.) It already had a building for the ceramic business and it was also very close to a Metro Link stop, which meant an easy access to the airport in the event that Dan would have to travel for a consulting position. The location was also a very easy drive to St. Louis, if needed. Could we have looked a bit longer and found something nicer and bigger, in a more prosperous area of town? Probably so, but we were afraid of not finding something so convenient, with a building and no deed restrictions. We didn't want to lose this nearly perfect place while we continued to look around for the home of our dreams. I was anxious to be home, so we bought it right away. Now the biggest drawback in this whole plan was that Dan could not retire until January 2004. I would have to initially move on my own. No problem, I had done it when we moved from Texas to Wisconsin, a place where I knew no one or where anything was. I could certainly handle this. I was going home! And, I would get to really pursue my ceramic business in my own building on my own property. Life was looking good. Things were happening like they were supposed to, or so I thought! We listed our home in Kenosha and the moving process began.

I was home near Mom. She was still working full time at Bridal Originals, so we spent many evenings together, as well as weekends while Jim was over in Missouri at his girlfriend's house. Some weeks I drove back to Kenosha to visit Dan and to bring back another van load of items. Some weekends Dan drove here with his pickup loaded with stuff. This was certainly one long slow move!

I tried to spend as much time with Mom as possible. I would scour the paper for events that we could attend together. I looked for craft shows and other community activities. On weekends when there would be several options to choose from, Moms favorite response was always, "Honey, you can't do it all."

A friend, who owned a ceramic mold business in the area, felt that we could become more viable than just a home based business. He connected us to a woman who had a large scale bisque supply business and she was wanting to retire and was looking for someone to take over her customer database. You know what they say about, "if it sounds too good to be true.!!!!" I was reluctant, but Dan saw it as the opportunity we were looking for. It was meant to be ours. We rented her building, fully stocked, with an established customer data-base; she and her staff of four all retired, but said that they were a phone call away and willing to help with questions.

OUR MOVE BACK TO ILLINOIS

January 2004 Dan and I stood in the middle of a 20,000 sq. foot building with over 30,000 ceramic molds on shelves. The fax machine had continued to spit out orders during the two week Christmas holiday while the shop had been closed; papers were scattered all over the office floor! Customers from all over the U.S who were not aware that there was a change in ownership, were now waiting for their post-holiday bisque orders to be shipped. We looked at each other and wondered where to begin. How do we even sort out these papers scattered all around us, much less figure where to find the molds to produce the products? What is their shelving system? A few phone calls begging for help and a couple of hours of showing us around, we at least had a starting point and a vague idea of where to find the necessary molds for the orders.

Jim and Mom both offered to help part time and earn some extra money. But, we quickly learned that it wasn't enough and we had to hire even more help. Very soon after that, Bridal Original's closed and Mom was out of a job. She came to the shop every day at 11:00 a.m. and worked until about 4:00 p.m. She would go home to fix supper for Jim when he got home from his day job. After supper they would both return so Jim could work a few hours. Mom counted and tracked the paint inventory; she priced the bisque and put it on the shelves. She loved talking to the various customers that came in and soon got to know the regulars quite well. One shop owner named Donna, often brought her Mother in with her to buy supplies. My Mom and Donna's Mom would walk around together and chat non-stop. Mom would show her the new stuff she had just put out on the shelves. I loved having Mom there every day, spending time with her. Even though there were many things I had to re-do after she left, it was worth it to me, to have her close and sharing our world.

There were several of my regular customers, as well as the owner of the building, who at various times each asked if Mom had Alzheimer's. It seems that each of them were going through it with their own Mothers. A couple said they could see it in her eyes. One asked about medications, such as Aricept® and that she should get on it now, to slow the disease down.

Mom was still not at the point to ever admit that she had a memory problem, much less to even think about mentioning the "A" word! The subject had to be approached very, very gently. I knew she would be very mad if she thought I had ever been talking about her to other people. So I turned it around. One day after her elderly friend had left and we were eating lunch, I told her that Donna had just told me that her Mom had Alzheimer's disease. Mom looked at me in wide- eyed surprise, exclaiming that she looked fine to her. I told her that she had been tested early and was on medication to slow it down; and that she is doing very well, but early testing was very important.

I did not tell Mom that I had been told by Donna that her Mother had also started fighting showering and washing of her hair. That Donna would often talk her into playing, "beauty shop" and washing and fixing each other's hair and doing their nails. So I had a hint of what to expect down the road.

As time went on, a lot of different things were happening and crashing in all at once. I found myself having double orders of some colors of paint, and completely out of others, I was also having to change the prices on most of the bisque, but I did these things when she wasn't around. Some days she would not show up at the expected time. When I called to check on her, she said she was busy or that she didn't need to tell me what she was doing, that I wasn't her keeper. Jim was losing interest in working the second job and often did not come to work as regularly as he once did. Neither Mom, nor Jim looked at our business as a real job; they did not look at us as employers. I was their daughter and sister.

They did not feel the need to call and let us know that they were not coming in as expected. We were on a downhill slide for sure. We still had not sold our house in Kenosha and we were dipping very deeply into savings accounts just to keep the business afloat and to keep Mom and Jim in part time jobs. We finally had to make the decision to release the building for sale, downsize the business and bring it home to our smaller building. Still providing Mom with a small part time job, where she felt needed and earning a small income. Jim we could no longer support.

We kept one other employee who assisted with the actual production end of the business. Mom continued to count paint and pull paint orders, and would also go with me to make local deliveries. We turned delivery days into outings that included lunch, shopping trips, or picnics in the park.

This downsizing was actually a decision made too late. Still not being able to sell our house in Wisconsin and neither Dan nor I were having any luck finding a job, we had no other choice but to file for bankruptcy.

It was 1961, I was nine years old. The Shrine of Our Lady of the Snows had recently opened. I made many trips there with Pop and Grandma (my Mother's parents.) I have wonderful memories of outdoor Masses at the Grotto and the ringing of the Angelus Bells reflected in the pool of water, where I threw in the change that Grandma had given me from her pocketbook. I especially remember the large outdoor Stations of the Cross. Fourteen large wood and stone display boxes with a glass front. Statues inside each box replicating the final days in the life of Christ on his journey to Calvary. There was a button at each station to push and listen to the story being depicted by the statues inside. Pop was too sick with colon and prostate cancer to walk the path, so Grandma drove her big red, 2 door, 1958 Plymouth along the way. At each station, Pop would open his door and I would slip out from behind his seat and go push the buttons so he could hear the stories. Even as a very young child, I remember it being a pretty special place to be with Pop and Grandma.

As an adult, the Shrine took on an even greater meaning as I grew to know what it truly represented in my own spiritual life. Driving through the front entrance was always breathtaking to me, not only in the true natural beauty of the place, but I felt the weight of the world lifted from my shoulders every time I entered. I always felt a sense of peace and tranquility in my heart. During the many years that we lived out of state, a visit back home to the metro-east was not complete for me unless I had paid a visit to the Shrine.

Now, I have just been hired to work in the gift shop! I now have the privilege of working here! I am being paid to be a part of this living memory! Every day as I pass through the entrance, I thank God for letting me be a part of this inspiring place, for providing this job at a time when I not only desperately needed the income, but I also needed solace. For a few hours every day, I can put my personal hell aside and let the positive energy of this place bring me some much needed comfort. I know in my heart that God truly provided the perfect job at the perfect time.

The job at The Shrine of Our Lady of the Snows was a God-saving moment in my life. It was the answer to so many prayers. I will be eternally grateful to the gift shop manager and staff who unknowingly helped me through so many of my darkest days.

Working in the Shrine gift shop gave me the opportunity to meet people from all parts of the world. I met priests and nuns from all corners of our state and beyond. It was very enlightening to witness the cultures and traits of other countries, young and old, caring and sharing. There were so many people with problems much bigger than mine, all turning to the Shrine and the mysterious workings of God to bring them comfort. Often times, a book would bring them the solace that they were searching for. One evening while helping a customer, I spotted my first book on dealing with Alzheimer's disease, *"Walking Each Other Home, Moments of Grace and Possibility in the Midst of Alzheimer's"* by Rita Bresnahan. I bought the book and read and re-read the book many times over, often reading into the wee hours of the morning, finding comfort, and fear at the same time. Reading her book, was almost as if someone was putting their hand on my shoulder and telling me what was about to be happening in my world.

During the next several weeks, one name in particular kept coming up, Fr. Stan Konieczny. Various customers would come into the gift shop looking for cards and gifts for the soon to be ordained new priest, everyone speaking with such delight of his personality, his warmth and sincerity. Even my Mom spoke of him almost weekly, as he was temporarily under the guidance of her priest, Fr. Ray Schultz, at Holy Trinity. Mom really liked this "older" man who was becoming a priest. I wondered if it had anything to do with the fact that he talked of Chicago with her. Anyone who knew anything of Chicago made Mom a happy lady. My curiosity was sparked, and I was certain that at some point the ever popular Fr. Stan would cross my path at the Shrine Gift Shop.

Dan finally found a consulting position, the downside being he would be traveling Monday thru Thursday, home only on the weekends. We adjusted our schedules and downsized the business again.

Any time that Mom did not show up at the usually expected time, I instantly worried, almost in panic. With great trepidation I would allow a bit of time to pass before calling to check on her.

One Sunday I had invited Mom to have brunch with Dan and me before he left on his business trip. The appointed hour had come and gone. I kept adding milk to the casserole to keep it from totally drying out. I finally decided to call and see if she was on her way. She answered the phone rather quickly. I asked what she was doing, to which she informed me that she was cleaning the ceiling fan in her bedroom because it was so dirty. I asked about her coming to brunch, and she said, "Yes, when it is time to come!" I told her that she was supposed to have been at my house an hour ago. She retorted back with, "I didn't know, you never tell me anything!" She arrived about 10 minutes later and all was fine. Dan had to quickly eat and leave.

One day when I called to see why Mom had not arrived to go on a delivery with me, she said she didn't have time for such nonsense; she had to clean the birdcage. Jim wasn't around to do it, and somebody had to!

On another day when she did not show up to assist with a scheduled delivery, I called and she answered right away, and quickly became agitated at me, saying that she did not need to report to me every day of what she was doing, but that if it was any of my business, she had a doctor's appointment, and couldn't come. Of course, I wanted to know if something was wrong and why was she going to the doctor. She told me it was just a regular check-up and that she was fine. She needed to see him in order to get her thyroid medicine refilled. Now my mind is racing, knowing that I could not rearrange my schedule on such short notice, and yet wanting to be with her and somehow let her doctor know of some of my recent concerns. I needed him to be aware of her recent behavior, I wanted validation. I called his office to see if I could speak to him. I was told, "No," but that I could send a fax and they would see that he got it before Mom's appointment. So that is exactly what I did. I started the message with: *"I am well aware of the current privacy laws, and realize that you are not able to discuss my Mom's medical records with me, but I want to inform you of some recent issues that I have noticed, your evaluation would be greatly appreciated. I also trust that the privacy law is a two way street and that you will handle this matter discreetly. I have a small ceramic business that Mom helps out with; she pulls my paint orders. The paint is stored in one small room in my basement. Yesterday while pulling a paint order for a customer, Mom started pacing, and looking around the room frantically searching for "something," when all of a sudden she loudly yells out, "DOESN'T THAT JUST FROST YOUR BALLS!" I looked at her in total shock. I had never heard anything like that ever come out of her mouth! She said, "Your Dad used to say that all the time." Well, maybe so, but Mom never did, Mom never said a cuss word of any kind, ever. Turns out she had misplaced the paint order sheet, and couldn't find it."*

Later that afternoon I received a phone call and the woman on the other end was furious with me for interfering in her business. She was screaming and yelling like I had never heard before. Her doctor had told her that I was concerned about her welfare. He asked her the usual preliminary questions of what was her address and phone number, what is today's date, and who is president of the United States. He told her that she was fine and that her daughter was probably over reacting. So much for privacy laws working on my behalf!

So now I felt I could not trust this doctor to be an ally on my behalf. If I could not talk directly to him and he would not take my input into consideration in his observations, what was I to do? My gut instinct was telling me that Mom was on a spiraling decline, she couldn't or wouldn't admit it, nor would she discuss any of the issues at hand. I was feeling helpless; I knew I needed help for myself as well as my Mother, but was unsure of where to turn for advice and help.

Mom continued to keep me on my toes, wondering how long could she really live on her own. When would Jim start realizing that her dementia was progressing? I learned the hard way that it was going to take a real tragedy for him to really accept what was happening.

Not long after the fax to the doctor incident, Mom called and asked about my doctor, wondering who and where I went, and could she change to him, so that we could go to the doctor together. While I was doing the happy dance and thanking God for having Mom make this decision on her own, without any prompting from me, I was also not going to take this phone call for granted. I needed to know why she suddenly made this decision. When I questioned this decision, she simply said that she thought that it was time for a change and since Jim was working now and would not be able to take her for office visits, she thought it would be best to go to my doctor. I also had to wonder, did she deep down in her own mind know that she needed more help than she was willing to ask for and that this was her way of reaching out for that help? I made all the arrangements, handled the paperwork and started taking her to my doctor. Now playing an active role in her healthcare, I could discuss with the doctor my concerns, we worked as a team. He gave Mom the standard evaluation tests, that included the basic questions of name, date, president, where are you, the drawing tests of a clock, and intersecting diagrams.

As before, Mom knew her name and address, she knew she was currently in Dupo, IL but her drawings of the clock and the interconnected boxes were very disjointed. The memory test of, "name 3 objects in the room," which had been previously pointed out, was completely lost on her. She was put on Aricept®. While I knew it was a major step in the right direction, I also knew it was most likely, too little, too late. But, at least I felt we were finally on the right track.

I received a very casual phone call one evening, Mom proudly announcing that she and Jim had been out and bought her a new car. *Really?? There was nothing wrong with her current car.* Oh yeah, she forgot to tell me that she had recently run into the back of a city bus and totaled her car; and that she had gotten to ride home in a police car! Really?? NO ONE! Not Mom, nor Jim thought it was important enough to tell me about it, when it happened? She didn't go to the hospital or doctor, she said she was fine! Did she really need to be driving? And now ……a new car???? I couldn't believe what I was hearing! Could she really afford the car payments? Let alone be driving now? But nobody consulted me on the issue, it was already done!

While I LOVED my job in the gift shop and all of my co- workers, after almost a year I knew I would not be able to continue to work there much longer, with a weak back and neuropathy of the feet, it was becoming increasingly hard to stand for the hours required. God intervened and helped me again. After many weeks of hearing about the heartwarming and personable Fr. Stan, I finally had the honor of meeting him myself. He invited me to attend a Mass at the church he had just been assigned to, St. Augustine of Canterbury. The following Sunday, I pulled into the parking lot and was walking up the sidewalk, just as he walked out the door of the rectory. It was almost as if he was there to personally welcome me to his church. Imagine my excitement when I read the bulletin to learn he just happened to be looking for a new part time secretary! Yeah, a sit down job! A coincidence? I think not! I believe that it was a God wink! I interviewed with him, the parish council, and the school principal, Sr. Bernadette Miller, (Sr. B) all of whom became an extended family to me. Like I had said earlier, you never knew who you were going to meet in the Shrine Gift Shop!!

Prior to becoming Fr. Stan's secretary, and a member of the parish, I had spent the previous couple of years searching for a parish to call home. I had tried and tested many of the local parishes. While I had nothing against any of them or their priests, I never felt "at home" like I did from the very first moment that I walked into St. Augustine's.

Almost two years earlier, one Sunday, while attending one the various churches during my searching for a parish to "call home" period, I was feeling completely overwhelmed, at what an undertaking my life had become. Feeling sorry for myself, wondering just what had I really gotten myself into with this move home; I had two homes in two different states, the business that had overnight become ten times bigger than I had ever imagined, or desired. I had several employees counting on us for their salaries, including a young man about to become a first time Dad. And then, there was the worry of Mom, and where we were going to be led as time went on. I knelt with my eyes closed and praying quite hard for the strength to get through this, and to not let anyone down. There were so many people counting on me at that point. The organ began to play and the choir started to sing, *"Here I am, do not be afraid. I am standing right beside you."* I could not control the tears suddenly running down my face, I knew those words was meant just for me! God was speaking directly to me to through the choir. That song never left my head the rest of the day, and has been a part of my daily life ever since.

As parish secretary, I received early notice of local events for inserting into the weekly bulletin. One that specifically caught my attention was that the Shrine would be hosting a music event; one of the guests would be singer/songwriter Tom Booth. I immediately marked my calendar for the event. I could not wait to see the man who wrote the song, which had moved me to tears and had become so important in my life. When the day arrived, I was quite honored to be able meet Mr. Booth and share my story of what his song has meant to me.

4

THE RIDE IS PICKING UP SPEED

In 2007, the ceramic business has been downsized to a point where I only have a few regular customers who pick up their orders on an appointment only basis, the custom candle holders that are shipped monthly to a company in Kansas City, and couple of craft shows. We still carry two different paint lines, but I am able to keep the inventory myself. We have sold off our bisque supply business, and have had to let all employees go, including Mom. Dan's current consulting position is based in St. Louis and he is home full time now and I am working part time as the parish secretary at St. Augustine's Parish in Belleville.

It is exciting and wonderful having the new job in the parish office, meeting so many new people and learning the behind the scenes operations of running a parish. I had no idea of the amount of work and time that it takes to keep a parish running. As a young girl in Cahokia, I went to a Catholic grade school and we went to Sunday morning Mass, but we were just pew fillers on Sunday mornings. We never participated in any activities or fund raisers of any kind. We never bonded with anyone outside of saying "Good Morning" and "Hello" to those around us as we came and went. My Grandma Wayne, on the other hand, was involved in every organization, volunteered wherever needed, baked cakes and cookies for bake sales, and tended to the needs of her many friends. I loved being her shadow at every opportunity, learning to make those decorated sugar cookies, helping and meeting people. I didn't know then that she was molding me to be a participating member of the church and our community.

As I became a Mom and my kids were in school, I was an active part of the PTA and a homeroom Mom, taking care of the parties and helping with each of the fundraisers. The girls were involved in scouting and the American Legion Junior Girls Auxiliary; this meant even more activities and fundraisers. At any given time my living room held candy, cookies, candles, calendars, or any other item that had been sold and awaited delivery. There were always treats being baked for various bake sales, and craft projects for the ongoing events taking place. Dan and I organized, built and manned Nacho and Watermelon stands for our local community picnics. The girls played elves for "Breakfast with Santa" at church; they were involved in the Clown Ministry Group, visiting nursing homes. I headed up the creating of a new large ceramic Nativity set for the church foyer. With each new activity, my Mom could always be heard saying to me, "Honey, you can't do it all."

Now, as I am learning the duties of the parish secretary, and all that it entails, and loving every minute of it; I am still holding on to the ceramic business and balancing my time with my husband and home, as well as Mom, and getting her to doctor's appointments and such. Am I feeling a bit overwhelmed? ABOLUTELY! But I think I have to do it all, because, who is going to help?

At this time, Jim is currently working for a temp service and has been working at various jobs at different times, mostly cleaning offices after their close of business, so therefore most evenings and nights, he is at work. The worst time for a dementia patient to be alone is after sunset. Many suffer from what is called "sun-downers" becoming restless and agitated in the evening hours. Of course Jim was not around to witness or even be aware of what was happening in her world. I could not be there every minute of every evening, but I did try to keep very close tabs on her.

Since retiring from Bridal Originals, all of the ladies had taken to meeting once a month for dinner at various places around town, in order to stay connected and keep up with each other's lives. I became part of the group, since I was Mom's chauffer for these nights out since she didn't like to drive at night any more. I enjoyed getting to know these ladies who had been Mom's co-workers for so many years. They knew her on a different level than the life that I shared with her. I enjoyed being able to observe her with her friends and see her as someone's friend and not just a Mom. She joked and teased and laughed with them. This was a side of my Mother that I had never seen. It was also enlightening to observe her friends beginning to notice the difference in her mannerisms. She didn't quite contribute to conversations like she once had. She mixed up facts from previous dinner conversations.

The dinners were the first Wednesday of the month. For me, Wednesday at work was the most stressful day of the week. It was the day that the bulletin had to be completed and submitted for publishing. It meant that no matter how busy the phone or the front door, the bulletin had to be completed. I usually left the rectory quite drained and just wanting to go home to my couch. But, the dinner night was something that I had begun to look forward to. It was nice having dinner with the ladies and spending quality time with Mom. It was good to see her out with her friends. I would call as I was leaving work, to let her know that I was on my way to pick her up. Sometimes she argued with me, that is was not the right day of the week, dinner is tomorrow, not today. She would yell that I never tell her anything, and why did I wait until the last minute and not give her time to get ready, even though we had discussed it the evening before, and again when I called her during my lunch; but by the time I picked her up, she was in a great mood and ready to go out to eat.

5

THE EVENTS OF 2008

I had taken Mom to a routine doctor visit on July 3, 2008, in Dupo, IL and then out to lunch. On this particular day we went to Oliver's at the Cahokia Airport. We have always enjoyed going there, to sit by the windows and watch the planes land and take off. She ordered chicken strips and french fries. I couldn't help but chuckle as I watched her eat. Like a kid staking her claim, she took a bite out of a chicken strip and set it down, then picked up a french fry and ate it. Then picked up a different strip and took a small bite out of it, set it down and ate another fry. This continued until she had taken a bite out of each and every chicken strip. It wasn't long before she said she was full. I told her we would get her a box so she could take the rest of them home with her for later. She said, "OK." Then next to her plate she spread out her used paper napkin and with the palm of her hand she flattened and straightened out every wrinkle. She pressed it with her hand as if she had an iron and was pressing a shirt. Before I knew what was happening, she had picked up her plate and dumped her chicken strips and fries in the middle of the neatly pressed napkin, and was rolling it into a tight little ball. *"Gee whiz, kids are quick!"* I told her the waitress was bringing her a box. And she said "OK". The box came, and the neat little paper ball was placed inside!

A few weeks later, I received a call from the doctor's office saying that Medicare had denied the charges of the office visit. I would need to call Medicare and find out why. Since I did not have a Power of Attorney yet, I had to go to Mom's house to make the call, so she could get on the line and give her permission for them to talk to me. When I made that call, Medicare said it had been cancelled effective June 1, 2008, that she now had GHP insurance. I was very fortunate to have gotten a very caring Medicare representative who went above and beyond what I have been accustomed to when talking to with any customer service representative, from anywhere! She walked me through the events of what most likely had happened and what would now need to happen to get Mom reinstated with Medicare. Normally, changes are in effect for a year before they can be changed back again, but since this had happened so recently and it was caught so quickly, and taking into consideration Mom's dementia, limited income and Social Security we should be able to get her Medicare reinstated. (*It was also during this phone call that I learned that the Medicare Health Plan premium is automatically deducted from Social Security Benefits. I did not know this before now. I realized that I was about to learn a lot; I was about to take a crash course in Medicare, Social Security, Elder Law and who knows what else would be coming my way!*)

The woman explained that most likely a sales person had come to Mom's door and said that he needed to discuss her insurance and had enough information with her doctor's name and her health problems. The very kind Medicare person stayed on the line and coached me on what questions to ask of Mom, trying to figure out just what had happened and when.

Just as she had expected, a man had come to the door and said that due to her having high cholesterol and that Medicare did not pay the full price of an office visit or medications, he was there to offer her a plan that would keep her from having to pay such high out of pocket expenses. Mom said that, "Since he was a nice young Catholic man, she felt it was safe to let him in the house." But insisted that she did not purchase any new insurance, the man had only given her a quote and he was supposed to come back and get her decision later. She went into the living room and came back with a booklet to show me what he had told her, and right there in the back of the booklet was the completed application with her signature. Needless to say, she did not know what she had signed. But it came down to; she had made GHP her primary insurance, with Medicare as her secondary. GHP had not paid anything on her doctor bill; since I did not know her insurance had changed and Mom certainly didn't know, and as she thought she had only gotten a quote, how was the doctor to know to bill them? How were any of us to know that GHP was her new insurance carrier? *("The nice young Catholic man" who came to the door? How did she know he was Catholic?)*

After a discussion with Fr. Stan, he surmised that most likely, the sharp eyed salesman noticed the Crucifix hanging on her wall; he knew what buttons to push and what to say to gain her confidence.

Now it was suddenly becoming clearer why a few days earlier she had complained about picking up a prescription at the drugstore and that the price had went up considerably. It seems that a prescription that for months she had only paid $10.00 and now all of a sudden it was $150.00. That was quite a jump. Again, I went to Mom's house to use her phone so she could give GHP permission to talk to me. I contacted GHP and they said that the claim for the doctor and the prescription had not been turned into them for payment. I proceeded to submit bills to them, canceled their service and got the Medicare reinstated. After spending many, many long hours on the phone, the issue was straightened out. However, GHP never paid for the prescription or the doctor. They ignored every letter and never returned any phone call.

I knew the day had come that I had to convince Mom to let me have Power Of Attorney, so that I could handle these matters without so many hassles. We had talked about it from time to time, but Mom was never ready to discuss it. Somehow, I would have to convince her it needed to be done. This was not going to be easy. Mom was very independent and I knew she would think that I was trying to take over her life. I would have a very hard time getting her to understand that I was merely wanting to help.

Mom called one afternoon just as excited as a young teenage girl in love with her first boyfriend. She was so happy that Richard had found her again after all of these years. She told the most amazing story of how her youngest granddaughter Julie, who lived in Effingham, had called her saying that her new art teacher had known her from when she had lived in Chicago. That he was her boyfriend when they were in high school. He went on to tell Julie that when her Grandma moved away from Chicago, he had never forgotten her. *(While I thought this was one of the most beautiful love stories I had ever heard, I also wondered how much was real. I accepted the story as she told it, but with reservations.)*

October 2008

As the wedding of my nephew Ray was approaching and Mom and Jim were making plans to attend the wedding in Effingham, stories of Richard escalated and became the focus of most of our conversations. In the latest conversation, she informed me that Julie had invited Richard to come to the wedding so he could see his former girlfriend once again. Mom was so excited, she had gotten out her senior picture that she had never had the opportunity to give him so many years earlier. She signed the back of it with, "Much Love to Richard, Virginia."

It was time for me to do some research and find out what was true and what was not.

Having been in contact with Mom's younger brother Jerry, as well as her best friend Marge, in Chicago, I did indeed learn that Richard had been her first true love. Richard and my Uncle Jerry played on the same neighborhood ball team, which is how Richard and Mom met. They dated and went to dances together. Upon graduation from high school, Mom's parents made her move with them back to Cahokia, where her Dad would be starting a new job as the maintenance man at the newly built Cahokia High School. She left Richard behind and they each went their separate ways. Shortly after the family moved, Richard and a couple of friends were hitch-hiking to California. Richard was hoping to pursue his dream of being an artist for Disney. On their trek across the country, they stopped for a couple of days in Cahokia to visit with her. That was the last time she ever saw him. I learned from Mom's friend Marge that he did not get the job as a Disney animator, but he did have a career as an art teacher in Chicago, later he and his wife retired somewhere in Arizona.

Next, I talked to my sister about Julie's new art teacher in Effingham. As I had suspected, Julie did not have a new art teacher, nor had she made any phone calls to Mom with such stories. I filled them in on the stories I had been told, and that Mom would be expecting to see Richard at the wedding.

At about this same time, we had a regularly scheduled doctor's appointment for evaluation to see if the Aricept® was having any effect on her. When the nurse started asking the usual questions of: what is your name, your address, today's date, who is the president? Draw this clock for me. Name the three objects in the room that were mentioned earlier. Mom proclaimed, just how stupid she thought this test was. "Why are you asking me such stupid questions? I have never had a test like this before!" The nurse said that they had done this at the last visit. Mom let her know in no uncertain terms, that she had NEVER done anything like this before, and this was the most stupid thing ever! After her little outburst, the nurse took Mom down the hall to try to get a urine sample from her. The doctor and I chatted and I told him the story about Richard and the upcoming wedding, and that Mom expected him to be there. I explained that Richard is not real at this present time, but had been very important in her past. We discussed the need to get a neurologist involved and get some MRI's run.

Needless to say, Mom was heartbroken that Richard did not show up at the wedding. "He must have been busy taking care of his elderly father, who is a very sick man, he is such a good son." This is how she explained him not being at the wedding.

(There is a part of me that wishes I could find Richard and let her see him one more time, but the reality is that she would not know this 80 year old man. This Richard would not be the 18 year old boy of her memories.)

It was a damp, grey, chilly fall day. A light rain has been falling all day. It is the kind of day that reminds you that winter will be here soon. It was late afternoon when my phone rang. Mom says, "I thought I should tell you that I had a small fender bender today. I asked her to explain what she meant by fender bender. She said that she was driving home from the store and her glasses fogged up from the rain, and she pulled over to clean her glasses so she could see. When she pulled over, she hit a curb. She was not hurt and there was just a little bit of damage to the car. I asked her describe the damage. She said there was a small hole near the end of the fender. I asked her what she had hit. She said, that she had only hit the curb; she does not know how the hole got there. So of course, I headed over there to be sure that she was OK and to see what the damage looked like.

She was fine and quite adamant that she had only hit the curb, though she could not remember exactly where. When I looked at the car, I knew it had to be something much taller than a curb! The hole was on the fender above the tire! I could see inside to the engine. I could see the engine and the windshield washer container. There was a huge piece of the fender hanging loose. Whatever and where ever she had hit, there had to be damage, as well as pieces of black plastic from her car. Jim tied up the loose hanging piece of fender with a bungee cord. He said he had been up and down the road to look for the missing car parts, but did not find anything.

She refused to let me call her insurance company since it hadn't been that long ago since her last wreck. She needed estimates done to see what it would cost to have it repaired by a friend of Jims. I drove her around to several auto body places, at each one, we got the same response. "What did you hit?" Mom was getting quite agitated that no one believed her when she said she had hit a curb. She would start yelling at each adjuster, "I didn't hit anything! It was just a curb!"

Quite some time after the incident, I learned that it had been a mailbox, but Mom never did remember where or how it had happened. Turns out my brother had discovered the downed mailbox, but had neglected to let me know about it.

All the estimates came in around $3,000. Knowing Mom did not have that kind of money, we turned to Jim's friend who had offered to fix it. He was now too busy and did not have the time. I told her it was not safe for to drive it like it was. I told Jim to hide the keys until we could figure something else out.

November 2008

Mom had an appointment with the neurologist that had been recommended to us. Immediately, Mom did not like this lady doctor, and in the back of my mind, I figured it was because Mom knew she could not "hide" from her. That one way or another, this lady doctor would figure her out. I was comfortable with her and knew that she would see through Mom's stories. She would ask Mom more than the usual questions, of what is your name, who is president, what is today's' date? She actually "talked" to Mom and tried to get to know who she was. Mom knew the answers to all of these questions, but the harder questions about what is really going on in her world, Mom resented. I encouraged Mom to tell the doctor about Richard. She stiffened her back, glared at me, as she shouted out, "**She doesn't want to hear about Richard!**" I had flipped the switch that let the "real her" out! The doctor picked up on this right away and said she would like to hear about Richard. "Is he your friend?" Then Mom softened and went right into her story of how Richard was her friend in Chicago and that they used to go dancing together.

He is now here and teaching art and he comes to visit and they dance. The doctor looked at me; I shook my head no. She nodded in agreement and asked Mom more questions that kept her talking of her friend Richard. The neurologist added Seroquel® to Mom's med list. She said it would help with the delusions. She also ordered a baseline CT scan of the brain.

The doctor asked her if she had a Will, and Power of Attorney papers set up. When Mom said she did not, the doctor in a very pleasant and agreeable tone, suggested that it would be a good idea. Everyone should have one, because in the event of an emergency, it would be too late. The doctor gently continued to explain to Mom, "Your daughter will need to know what your wishes are later on, when you are unable to speak for yourself, and that even if she knows, legally, she cannot follow through with them, if she does not have the Power to do so. You really should see a lawyer and have it put in writing legally, so Carolyn will be able to take care of important things for you." Mom replied with her usual, "OK." Which made me wonder if the doctor had made any real impact on this fact or not.

We were scheduled to come back in about 6 weeks to follow up.

On the car ride home, Mom brought up the subject of the Power of Attorney and wondered how to get one. I hesitated; I knew I would only have one chance to make it happen and I could not blow it. I kind of played dumb and said I did not really know, but that I was sure that her cousin Mearl would know how to get one. Her face lit up, she said, "YES! I'm sure he does! I will have to call him" (*Okay, that went well, now I hope she does follow through!)*

We went to lunch at the Pie Pantry for a sandwich and a piece of pie. When I dropped her off at her house, the last thing she said was that she was going to call Mearl.

Mearl is Mom's cousin, and he is the St. Clair County sheriff. She has told me stories of when they were kids, how he was her protector. As adults, his busy life and her duties as a wife and Mom did not allow for much interaction, but she always spoke very highly of him. Of course, she called on him for advice whenever the need arose. He was always there to offer whatever help he could give. I had to hope that she would make the call, and if she did, I knew he would advise her to get the legal matters taken care of.

We said our goodbyes and I drove home.

I was not in my house 10 minutes, when she called me. She had talked to Mearl; and he had given her the name of a nice young attorney who would be able help to her. She wanted to give me the number so I could schedule the appointment for a time that would be good for me.

Thank you, Dear Jesus!
Again, You have answered my prayers!

I called the attorney's number that was given to me. At the initial visit, he first explained that POA's and Wills were not his normal line of law, but he was glad to help, since we were related to the sheriff. He then proceeded to explain to Mom, that we would need to draw up several different sets of papers. He explained that she would have to think about a lot of things before we would actually write up the real papers. I liked that he explained things in terms that she could understand. First would be the Power of Attorney for handling the sale or purchase of her property and finances; including her retirement benefits, Social Security and any insurance policies that she may have. She would have to be sure that she trusted that I would act only in her best interest.

Then we discussed the Power of Attorney for Medical. He explained to her that this would give me the power to make any and all medical decisions, if she became unable to make the decisions for herself. Then there was the Last Will and Testament where she would need to decide how to divide up her personal belongings to her children and grandchildren. He gave her samples of each of the documents so she could take them home and read them and think about what she wanted to do.

Because of both mine and the attorney's schedules and the approaching holidays, we set a follow up date for after the first of the year.

December 24, 2008

I picked Mom up to attend an early evening Christmas Eve Mass at her church, Holy Trinity in Fairview Heights, and then dinner before I would go to Midnight Mass at my own church, St. Augustine of Canterbury in Belleville. When she came out to the car, she was wearing a long black skirt, black hose, black shoes and a long black coat. When I told her that she looked like a nun, she took it as a compliment, she laughed as she then continued to tell me that she had to go back at the last minute to change her shoes, because she could not get her coat on over those shoes, they were too big. When I questioned how her shoes affected her putting on her coat, she repeated that the shoes were TOO BIG!

I do not know what the coat had to do with the shoes, but I let it be; there was no point to continue on with the issue. I was learning to pick my battles. Some things were just not worth trying to make sense of, or to try and prove a point. It is what it is.

**June 1, 1975 –
25th Wedding Anniversary
Claude & Virginia
Linda, Bob, Jim, Carolyn**

6

THE EVENTS OF 2009

Throughout this coming year, we toured and visited many different Assisted Living Facilities. I knew that this would be the year that the move would have to be made; I also wanted Mom to be a part of this decision making process. She needed to have some say in where she was going to live as long as she was able to do so. We took our time; I never made it a mission of something that needed to be done in a week or two. It took us several months of searching. It was a lot like Goldilocks looking for that right bed to sleep in. Some were not as clean as I would have liked, some, while being clean were quite old, and had that "old hospital" feel. We found nothing that a person would want to call home. Another one, while being very, nice was way out of our price range, as well as others had hidden fees that were not readily found until further investigation. I always made sure that either Dan or Jim went with us when we went to tour a place. I was afraid to go by myself, afraid of what would happen if she turned on me and became uncontrollable. I also had hoped that somehow Mom would realize that we were all in this together. That I alone, was not making these decisions. There were a couple of times I was glad to have the extra help; as she did have a few little flare ups, but not too badly. We also turned each visit into an outing with lunch or dinner and some shopping.

It was while touring one of the facilities that I learned that Mom could be entitled to VA benefits as the spouse of a deceased veteran. I called and made an appointment to talk to an administrator of the benefit plan. I gathered up all of the necessary documents to prove when Dad had served in the Air Force. During the meeting I was asked about the equity in her home. I told him that the home was no longer in Mom's name, that she had put it solely in my brother's name several years earlier. He asked about stocks and CD's. I said there weren't any; she had cashed everything in quite some time ago in order to help my brother with his bills. He asked about life insurance policies, I told him that she had apparently sold them all. I could find no evidence of any current life policies. As it turns out, yes, she is qualified for VA benefits due to Dad's service time;

however, VA benefits take a long time to go into effect. She would need enough money to pay the fees of a nursing or assisted living facility for at least 6 months before the benefits would start. Also with the amount of her retirement and Social Security and no home in her name, and no insurance or CDs' she qualified for state aid, since she was considered at the poverty level. He went on to say that she could not collect both state aid and VA benefits, and that under her circumstances, she would be better off with state aid.

While being informative, it had turned into a dead end for us.

February, 2009

Mom and I returned to the attorney's office. She had her sample Power of Attorney for Property papers completely filled out, and her list of possessions neatly and precisely written down on a piece of paper. She told him though, that she had questions and was unsure on the health papers. I was proud, that she was able to still be able to give this some thought. It showed me that she was still able to do some thinking for herself, and I think this also helped to prove that she was still of sound mind and body and able to legally be making these decisions.

Her thoughtful questions helped to ease my own doubts and fears.

March 13, 2009

Our youngest daughter, Danielle, had arrived from CA, to help celebrate Dan's 60th birthday. This week turned out to bring forth many revelations to us. Dani's first day in town, she wanted to spend with her Grandma. They went to dinner at Dani's favorite place, Cracker Barrel, and had then planned to go see a movie. However, when Mom gave her directions to the theater, they ended up miles on the other side of town, nowhere near any movie theater. This really worried us, since Mom did still drive to and from the grocery store, which really wasn't that far from the movie theater. Now we were wondering if she had gotten lost before and had never said anything.

During this same visit, one day Dani went over to her Grandma's house during the middle of the afternoon, to find her sitting on the couch having a deep conversation with some invisible person. Dani was not sure who she thought Grandma was visiting with, possibly Richard?

On another day, Mom called the house, wanting to know the name of the big movie place that Dan and I had taken her to a couple of times over in St. Louis. After a few questions, I figured out that she was thinking of the Fox Theatre over on Grand Ave., where we had seen "Phantom of the Opera," "The Rockettes' Christmas Show," "Wicked," and "The Rat Pack Tribute Show." She said Richard was at the house and they were looking for something to do. They thought they would go over there, but she could not remember the name of the place. I told her they were not open during the day, only at night. She said, "OK, we'll find something else to do." I called her right back and said that Danielle would like to come meet Richard while she is in town. Mom said, that would be fine, Dani jumped in the van and went right over there.

When Dani arrived, Mom was standing out in the carport waiting for her. She said Richard had left, that he had remembered that he needed to go home and take care of his Dad. She never let Dani in the house on that visit. She stood out in the carport and talked until Dani decided to leave.

In conversations with Danielle about this particular incident, we had to wonder, when does the logic of the here and now take over the fantasy of the delusions? How does one go from saying it is OK for the granddaughter to come meet her fantasy friend, then to snap into knowing that she cannot meet him, and then create the perfect excuse of why he had to leave? How does this work?

March 17, 2009

Mom and I were in our local grocery store buying the items needed for making a corned beef and cabbage dinner. While studying the selection of corned beef, standing next to us was a black woman with red hair and wearing a pair of bright green plaid slacks. Mom quite loudly states, "Oh yeah, like she is Irish!" The woman gave Mom a look of definite anger and shock. I apologized to her on Mom's behalf, to which Mom loudly asks, "What are you "Sorry" for? She's NOT Irish!" The poor woman shook her head and walked away. I wanted to crawl in a hole from embarrassment, yet I knew Mom did not know that she was hurting someone's feelings. The Mother that had raised me would have never been so vocal like that.

April 1, 2009

Mom and I returned once again to the attorney's office to finish up the paperwork. She was ready to sign the Medical Power of Attorney papers.

April 13, 2009

Mom's younger brother Jerry has arrived from Bettendorf, Iowa, for a long overdue visit. He was not able to attend her birthday party last year and had finally been able to make the trip. He and I have kept in touch by phone and I have kept him updated on Mom's declining memory. We are all sitting around her kitchen table talking and catching up. He mentions singing recently at his sister-in-law's funeral service. Mom looked at him in total surprise and asked him when did he start singing? And that she would like to hear him sing sometime. He kind of laughed, and said, "Why Sis, I have always sang, you've heard me." She said, **"N-0- 0-0, I have never heard you sing, no one ever told me you could sing!"**

As long as I can remember, if there was a local community or charity event, my Uncle Jerry was always invited to join in singing with whatever band was on stage. In fact, he even sang at my own wedding 43 years ago. This was an important fact that Mom no longer remembered.

While Jerry was here visiting, we went down to the jailhouse to visit with Mearl. Mearl asked Mom about the lawyer he had recommended to her; I thanked him for his help and also brought up that we had been looking into various assisted living facilities. He said that was a wonderful idea and that it would be great for her, and that he himself would be giving it some thought, as soon as he would decide to retire. *A very smart man!* He had planted a wonderful seed in her head! Because, if Mearl thought it was a good idea, then it must be so! She was now receptive to the idea; if only for the moment, it was something I could refer back to if need be.

April 15, 2009
Tonight was the monthly Bridal Originals retiree dinner. The ladies were all discussing their pension, retirement, and death benefit plans. Because they had all started and retired at different times, each of their contracts were slightly different and they were all making comparisons. When asked what she was getting for a monthly pension, Mom didn't know. When asked how long she had worked there or when she started working at Bridal, she didn't know. One of the ladies slipped me her phone number and said I should call her.

Which I did the next day, she wanted to give me the phone number for the benefits office, so that I could get needed information for myself.

June 1, 2009

This morning we had an early morning appointment for a CT scan of the brain. This would be the follow up to the initial scan to see if there have been any changes. She came out looking totally disheveled; her hair all askew, her eyes wide in fear, she said she would never do that again, this was awful. I saw the look of a totally terrified woman. "That machine just kept making an awful pounding sound…boom, boom, boom!" I said, "You had it done before and you didn't think it was so bad." She said she had NEVER had anything like this before. The last time she was here, they just checked her eyes. I tried to tell her that she had it done just a few months earlier, she became furious with me right there in the hallway and started yelling, **"NO I HAVE NOT DONE THIS BEFORE!!! NEVER, NEVER, N E V E R!!"** She was leaning in towards my face and shaking her finger at me. I was standing in the hallway of the hospital talking to woman who looked and acted half crazed. I will never forget the lost and wild look in her eyes that day. I tried to calm her and said, "OK, we won't have to do this again."

I said we would go out to lunch, in order to get her mind off the ordeal. It is getting harder and harder to hold a real conversation with her; I spend most of the time searching my own mind, trying to figure out just what we can talk about. I was also learning the fine art of redirecting her focus.

I realized that today was Mom and Dad's wedding anniversary. So I said, "Do you know what today is?" Of course she replied with a "No." I said, 'It is your anniversary. She said, "Anniversary, what anniversary?" I said, "Your wedding, when you and Dad got married." She responded with, "Oh phew, that, whatever!" I asked her how many years and of course she didn't know. As she gave a flip of her hand she said, "I quit counting that a long time ago. Other than my three kids, the rest of it, I would rather just forget about." *(Now I have to wonder, since Mom had four kids, who is she not counting? I have to believe that since my brother Bob has been dead for over 30 years, she has completely blocked out that painful memory. But then,*

the rational, or is it the irrational side of me has to wonder, does she NOT count me? Does she wish that I was the one not around, since I am the one making her do things and see doctors she doesn't think she needs? Does she know that I am her daughter, or who does she think that I am?

I am very aware that Mom has no concept of time. I spend two or three days a week with her and have tried to make it clear that in a couple of weeks I am going to go out to California to spend a few days with Danielle and Kane. This week, I missed one day of going over to visit her, and the next day, she wanted to know how my trip to California was. It is still another week before I would leave.

June 2009

I picked Mom up to take her to church; she is wearing a long sleeved sweatshirt. I told her that I thought she might get too warm in church in that sweatshirt, that it is very warm for June. She insisted she would be fine, because it was a thin sweatshirt fabric; and she knows if she is too hot or not, she didn't need me to tell her if she would be too hot! So I proceeded to drive to church. It is 96 degrees outside. As we are walking across the parking lot of Holy Trinity Church, a lady getting out of her car commented that she was going to be awfully warm inside, since the AC was not working. Mom responds with, "Oh, OK." And right there in the middle of the parking lot she pulls it up and over her head. Fortunately for everyone around she didn't put on any real show out in the parking lot, because she had on 2 more shirts under the sweatshirt! I thanked the woman who convinced her to take off the sweatshirt. She certainly would have been very warm with all of those layers on!

(Did Mom decide to take off the sweatshirt because the woman told her that the AC was not working, or did Mom accept the strangers words, because it was not me saying them? Did she have a moment of reality and realized it was warm? I will never know.)

Mom called and said, "Richard was just here, he was teaching the little girls next door how to draw. They love it when he comes over, they really like him."

(Even by this time in our ride, no one else is truly seeing what I have been seeing. I am still wondering, am I making too much of it, or am I the one going crazy; seeing and hearing things that no one else does? Why does she not act this way in front of them? Then I start thinking that maybe, just maybe, somewhere in the dark tunnels of Mom's mind, she knows that neither my brother nor sister will take the initiative to take on these responsibilities. Maybe she feels safe with me, she knows that I will step in and take charge. I will make the necessary phone calls and do what needs to be done. She would never dream of asking for help, but is the acting out, and mood swings with me, her way of reaching out for help?)

July 1, 2009

I tried to call Mom and learned that the phone had been disconnected. I drove over to the house and neither Mom nor Jim was aware that the phone was off. Of course, Mom had not paid the bill. She said she had, and she pulled out a check book register to prove it. Yes, in the register it did show that she had paid her phone bill, however, the register was from two years ago! She got real defensive and started yelling that she pays her bills. I managed to calm her down by telling her that there must be a problem with the bank and that we needed to go to the bank and get the problem straightened out. The mood switch suddenly changed; she was once again in a happy place, because now she is thinking that we can prove it was not her fault, it was going to be the banks fault that her phone was turned off. We went to her bank and got the printouts of her account, which I spread out on her table and went over with her. I showed her that she was 3 months behind in her house payment, 2 months behind in her car payments, her Home Owners Insurance was delinquent, and there were five overdraft fees on each month. I had no idea what all of the other the utilities looked like. There were also some reoccurring monthly withdrawals that she could not explain. I would have to figure those out later. I called the phone company from my cell phone and made arrangements to get her phone reinstated. I had to guarantee that all future payments would be made on line and I needed to put up $150.00 deposit.

I told Mom I was going to set up a new bank account, since the other one was in such a mess, I told her that we needed a new account so that those companies that were taking money out, and she did not know who they were, would not be able to take any money out of the new account. I told her that this is the only way we would be able to fix her bank account. She said OK, but did she really understand? *I don't think so.*

I went to the bank with my Power of Attorney papers. I transferred $300.00 to a new account, with a debit card in my name only, and set up on-line banking. (Since Mom and I had been in the bank quite frequently lately, they had gotten to know me and what the situation was that was unfolding in front of all of us. They were very co-operative with me whenever I called or went in.) The bank gave me the papers that Mom would need to sign in order to open our new joint account. At this stage, it was quite easy for me to slide papers in front of her and ask her to sign them. I explained it was for a new account that we had to set up at her bank, so I could pay her phone bill on line, or else the phone company would not let her keep the phone. She said, "OK," and signed the papers. I was so relieved and knew that this had been too easy and all days would not be like this. But I was grateful for this accomplishment!

The first blow came about a week later; she went to the bank to get some cash and they gave her a box of new checks that had my name and address on them. *(The new checks were supposed to have been mailed to my house.)* Mom called, she was mad as she could possibly be. She wanted to know why my name was on her checks! When I explained that it was for the new account for paying her utility bills, she just quietly said, "Oh, OK" and all was fine. She could get so mad one minute, and then immediately, just do a complete turnaround, and it was like nothing had been said.

I set about having her Social Security, retirement and insurance draws being direct deposited into the new account. This all took a lot of phone calls, countless numbers of faxes sent back and forth, and office visits with Mom usually in tow, or on the phone with me. In her mind, we were having to go through all of this mess, because her bank screwed up her account. She was mad that they had made this mess, and we were the ones having to do all of the work to get it fixed. I could not close the old account until I was sure that I had all monies going to the right account and that all debits could be accounted for and explained. This entire process took over four months to be successfully completed.

One monthly debit for $19.95 had me perplexed; the name listed on the bank printout did not come up when I did an internet search and Mom, nor Jim, knew what it was for. So, back to the bank to see if they could supply any more information. They gave me a name and phone number. Back to Mom's house to make the call, so she could authorize them to talk to me. Turns out it was a company who offered discounts on travel, hotels and admissions to various theme parks. OK, how did this get started? They said she requested it by cashing a check that had been sent to her. Of course, she knew nothing of what they were talking about, but we got it cancelled.

Several months later in my own junk mail, was a check. Reading the fine print on the back, it stated that by cashing this check I authorized them to take $19.95 a month out of my checking account for "fun discounts." Now it was clear how Mom's incident had happened. (*What 80 year old person with dementia, living in poverty is going to read the fine print on the back of a check? She saw that check as pennies from heaven and cashed it without giving it a second thought! The swindling company had been stealing from my poor Mother's bank account for months; and I wondered how many other elderly people fall prey every day to such thievery!)*

Father Stan's going away Party

Today, I was taking Mom to church with me for Fr. Stan's final Mass at St. Augustine's Parish, because he was being transferred to another parish. When she walked out of her door to come get in my car, I noticed that she had on two pairs of slacks, the bottom blue pair, being much longer than the top black pair. I asked her why, and she said she wasn't wearing two pair, the bottom was the lining and it was just hanging out. She would need to sew them later. She could not be convinced to go back in and change, or to remove one pair. She had already locked the door and she was not getting her keys back out. I would have to deal with this later. We arrived at the church hall; she went with me to take my dish in for the luncheon. At that time, I suggested we use the restroom in the hall before going over to the church. She was very agreeable. While she was in her stall, I asked her take off her extra pair of slacks and give them to me and I could put them in my purse. Immediately, and without comment, the extra pants were tossed under the door to me. Mission accomplished!! (*I had expected a sharp reply of "Fine!" or "There!" but she didn't say a word.*)

July 20, 2009

Talking to Mom on the phone, she casually mentions that there had been a small fire at their house earlier in the day, before Jim left for work. Thank goodness Jim was still home. She said she smelled something burning and then saw smoke coming from his fish tank in the living room. He came out of his room and noticed that there was smoke rolling about waist high throughout the living room. He unplugged the aquarium, opened the windows and doors and told her that the smoke should clear out pretty soon. He then left for work. Not a call to me or anything.

(Did I expect too much from him? If she had been alone, I know she would not have known what to do.)

When I questioned him later about the incident, he really thought it was not a big deal. He explained, that it was just a clump of crystallized salt that had fallen off the top of the tank and fell onto the power strip. He said that once he unplugged it, it was fine. (*Sadly he could not see the whole picture here, of what could have happened had she been alone.*)

July 21, 2009

For several months now, my husband had been planning a very special surprise anniversary get-a-way for our 40th anniversary. I knew we were going somewhere for an extended weekend, though I didn't know where or what the mode of travel would be. Now with so many events happening with Mom, I could not see how I could leave for a few days, on the other hand Dan was telling me that I needed to get away. I hated the idea of leaving Mom at home, totally alone with Jim and his disconnect of what was happening... Even if something serious happened, what would he do? Would he even call and let me know? He had never called about anything so far. I decided that it was time to bring my sister along on this ride too. Hopefully, Mom could stay at her house for a few days; and with Linda's grown kids, and all of their little ones in and out all the time, Mom would have plenty of eyes watching out for her.

Linda was the only one that Mom ever let cut and perm her hair and she was long overdue. So, that became the plan. Linda and her husband, Ray, would pick Mom up early on Wednesday morning to take her to their house, where she would stay until Monday. Mom was excited when Linda called and invited her out to her house for some special Mom/daughter time. On Tuesday evening, I was at Mom's and she was showing me her overnight bag that she had packed and was ready to go. She showed me the pajamas she had gotten for Christmas, from Jim and his girlfriend, and had rarely worn, it had a matching robe. She thought it would be very nice to take to Linda's house. She showed me the blouses and pants she was taking. She said she was looking forward to this. She had never been out to spend time at Linda's all by herself before. She was quite excited about her trip.

Wednesday morning, I met Linda and Ray at Mom's and gave them some gas money, as well as, a few extra dollars for doing this. All seemed to be going well; the overnight bag was on the table and ready to go. I had also just learned from Dan that he had rented a condo in Branson for the weekend, so I was at least able to tell them where I would be. I kissed Mom goodbye and told her to enjoy her weekend trip.

Dan and I arrived at a condo on a golf course. We were able to enjoy watching the players from our screened in porch. We went out to see a magic show, had dinner, and then bought some groceries for the weekend. The next day we went to Silver Dollar City. On Friday, Dan said he would just like to hang out at the condo and rest and watch movies. Sounded good to me, but what a surprise I had later that day when our daughter, Lisa, from Houston and her boyfriend, Scott, showed up! Our youngest daughter, Danielle, was supposed to have arrived with them, but due to Kane's recent bicycle accident and having two broken wrists, she had to stay home. After Lisa and Scott rested a bit, the four of us went out to a dinner and a show that Dan had pre-arranged. What a wonderful evening we had. Shortly after returning to the condo, the doorbell rings and there is our very dear friend, Debbie, and her boyfriend, Chris. What a surprise this was! Dan went to the closet and started pulling out boxes. He had packed our Wii game set, some board games and a complete bar supply. It was now time to party!

On Saturday, Debbie, Chris, Dan and I went back to Silver Dollar City, so that I could buy a painting from an artist that I had admired for years. He was going to be there doing signings.

Lisa and Scott, went grocery shopping so that Scott could prepare one of his very special baked Salmon dinners. After dinner, we were outside playing a game that Chris had brought. When it got dark it was time to go back inside for more Wii and table games. This was certainly a wonderful relaxing weekend shared with family and dear friends. Dan did a good job at planning this get-a-way. He does things like that!

In the meantime, back in Effingham, IL, Linda proceeded to give Mom the perm and haircut. While doing so, she noticed that Mom had a distinct odor, like that of a person who had not bathed in a while. After the perm, Linda told Mom she needed to take a bath. Of course, Mom did not think it was necessary. Linda proceeded to start running the bath water and told Mom that she had perm solution on her and she needed to get it washed off. Mom responded with, "FINE!" and then stripped naked right there in front of Linda. Now, this is something my Mom would never have done before! She was very modest and had always made sure that none of us had ever seen her without her clothes on. Linda went to get Mom some clean clothes out of the overnight bag, only to discover that there weren't any. The bag was filled with underwear, but no clothes or pajamas. Linda found some t shirts and pants of Julie's that Mom could wear. Mom must have repacked after I left her on Tuesday evening. I never thought to check her bag again before she left on Wednesday morning.

Linda called me several times during those couple of days. She and her family were getting a firsthand look at what Mom was going through and just how confused she was getting. The reality of my life was coming to them in ways that I could never have explained in our phone calls. Mom constantly followed Julie around like a little puppy. At one point, Julie thought she could occupy Mom by having her help make brownies, but Mom did not even know how to grease the pan.

Mom kept insisting that she needed to go home, that she had bills to pay, she had things she needed to do. Even though I was not due home for another day, Ray drove Mom home, to keep her from getting too upset. They were sure that she would be alight for one day by herself.

Prior to this weekend with Mom, there had been some tentative discussion of Mom moving out to Linda's, where there were more people around all of the time. I know this visit ended any such talk. They all realized what an undertaking it would be, and that it would not be fair to Julie to become Mom's babysitter.

August 2009

My life seemed to be spiraling out of control; as things started becoming clearer, more and more red flags were waving in front of me like beacons in the night. It seemed the more that I learned and realized what needed to be done, the more I knew I did not know WHAT to do. If I knew what needed to be done, HOW? It was quite obvious I was on my own; Linda and Jim both would just say "I don't know," "yeah," "hmmm,"

No input, no suggestions, no feedback. A real two way conversation did not exist. I always felt like I was talking to a wall, and expecting it to answer.

The bank that holds the title on the car has been calling saying that they can no longer accept Mom's random checks of $10.00 and $20.00. She is more than six months behind in payments; they either want to be paid in full or they will repossess the car. I told them to come take the car. She can't pay for it and doesn't need to be driving it. So, I let her know that the car would be picked up soon, since she was so far behind in her payments. Thankfully, she blamed the bank and how they had messed everything up.

I decided that I should contact our attorney to see what my obligations would be, in the event that, after the car is repossessed and sold, if there would be a balance due, what are my responsibilities as POA.

The attorney pointed out that this was not his area of expertise, but gave me the name of another attorney who would be able to answer my question. That attorney told me that I am not personally responsible; my Mom does not have the funds, she will soon be moving into assisted living and they will have the car to sell and they will just have to accept it and write off the difference. And I quote, the attorney said, "You can't get blood from a turnip."

It is a Wednesday night dinner out with the ladies from Bridal Originals. We are seated at a large table for about twelve ladies. Baskets of rolls are placed randomly on the table. Little ceramic crocks piled high with butter are also placed near the baskets. The ladies are reaching for the rolls, and, Mom reaches for the crock of butter, picks it up and proceeds to lick it like an ice cream cone. The ladies at our end of the table are looking at her and then to me, in total shock. I lean over to tell her that it is butter and it is supposed to be for everyone. She looks at me like I am nuts. With wide eyes and a look of defiance, she proceeds to lick the butter again, she says, "It's good!" The other ladies asked the waitress to please bring more butter.

August 11, 2009

I have been giving a lot of thought into asking Jim's girlfriend for some input into the situation. On one hand I am not sure I want her input, because of her overbearing personality and "know it all" mannerisms, but then again, I know she is a home healthcare nurse and very observant, and would give an honest opinion of her observations. When I asked, she said she has noticed that Mom is very confused and lost, and taking frequent naps. She has observed Mom "talking" to someone on the couch, (no one was sitting on the couch.) When we talked about Mom's meds and whether or not she was taking them properly, it became evident that Mom had not been taking her thyroid medicine. But my biggest problem with this entire conversation lies in the fact that she is a trained nurse and sits with other elderly people. She had been observing her boyfriend's mother, showing obvious signs of delusion and mental decline, and she did not feel the need to say anything to me. Had she said anything to Jim? If she did, he never relayed any of her concerns to me, but of course, he had never relayed any of his own concerns, if he had any. I will never understand why I had to be the one to inquire.

My biggest issue was that for several years she had been almost like a m e m b e r o f t h e family, and shared many family holidays and other events. Mom was not her patient, so privacy laws do not apply here. Her saying that she didn't think it was her place to say anything was purely uncaring on her part. Had she said something, we could have started seeking proper medical attention much sooner.

Because of my commitments to the annual ceramic show for the next two days, I would not be able to address this until Sunday. I was going to have to make her start using the daily pill reminder box, that I had bought and she refused to use. I discovered she was also out of Aricept®, but did still have some Seroquel® left. It turned out that she had not had the thyroid medicine filled since May.

August 15, 2009

It is about 7:00 p.m. on Saturday night, I have tried to call Mom to tell her that I would be over on Sunday morning after church to bring the prescriptions that I had picked up for her. There was no answer, so I left a message. Then, I decided to call Jim's cell and tell him. Just a very short time later she called me back, sounding very sleepy. She said she was quite tired and had slept in this morning and when she woke up, Jim told her that I had called. She wondered why I was calling so early in the morning. She got quite aggravated at me when I told her it was nighttime, not morning. It was time to be going to bed, not getting up. I told her I would be over the next day with her prescriptions. *(What was Jim doing? Did he try to help her realize what time of day it was, or did he just let her be? Did he even notice or care? I have no way of knowing what his thoughts are, he doesn't discuss them)*

August 16, 2009

As soon as I pulled into the driveway, she was out the door with her purse, ready to go. This is the first time EVER, that she has been ready to go anywhere with me. She said she was ready to go pick up the prescriptions, and was frustrated with me when I showed her that I already had them with me. I went straight to the cabinet and pulled out the pill reminder box that I had previously bought her, and she is obviously not using, since it was still in the package. I pointed out that her Aricept® bottle was empty and it was 5 days too early. I am wondering how early? A day or two, or much longer? I asked about her FOSAMAX®, she waved the package in my face, retorting, "SEE! It is all gone!" (*OH, MY GOSH!!! SHE HAS TAKEN A WHOLE MONTHS WORTH IN LESS THAN A WEEK! WHAT WILL THAT DO TO HER????)*

I looked at Jim and lost all self-control, I was absolutely livid and started yelling, **"Can't you see that she cannot take care of herself? She does not know day from night! She does not**

know when to take her meds! She cannot pay her bills properly! You are not helping at all, you are not aware of what is going on around you! You are behind in your house payments and it will soon be in foreclosure and then what will you do?"

Mom's voice quietly and calmly chimes in from behind me with, "Oh, it already is, I got a letter the other day." She trots off to the other room and brings back a letter to show me. The other day?? OH MY GOSH!!! This letter is dated June 30th; it is now the middle of August!!!!! The letter clearly states that they are in foreclosure. Jim said he was not aware of this at all. He said that he is not good at talking to people about these kinds of things, would I handle it? Since the house is in his name, he gave me his social security number and all other needed information, in order to try to rectify the situation. I am now delegated to contact the mortgage company on his behalf. Now I have another responsibility on my plate!

About this same time, Mom was asking to go back to her first doctor; she said that she liked him better. At first, I was hesitant, but after some thought, I decided that I had accomplished what had needed to be done to get her into the care of a neurologist, getting a diagnoses and the proper medication to help with her delusions and anxiety. While I knew I didn't have a great deal of respect for him and the way he had dismissed my very early concerns, if it would make her happier to see him again, I could not deny her that bit of control over this decision.

Our first visit back to her original doctor was my initial meeting with him. She had always said he was good looking. (I have an aunt and an uncle who also went to this doctor, and my aunt thought he was gorgeous!) Ok, he is very easy on the eyes, but that still didn't erase the fact that he had blown me off and ignored me in the beginning. My reservation level was still quite high. As he talked to Mom and inquired about things since they had last seen each other, he took great care in including me in the questions and his observations of the changes since she had been there last. I was warming up to this man, until he said, "I knew that she was showing obvious signs of dementia the last time she was here, but there has been a significant progression since then. I am glad you got her into a good neurologist. That will help a lot as we go along."

(Really?? You knew there were signs of

dementia?? You ignored my requests for help?? You told her I was overreacting??

My blood was reaching a boiling point right about now. I told myself that we would get through this; Mom was happy with him. If she was happy, then maybe her outbursts would not be as bad. She would still be in control of her medical choices with my supervision. Now that I would be with her at every visit, and that I was now listed as someone that the doctor could share information with, I could maintain a handle on the situation.)

As he continued to talk to Mom, he suggested that she look into an assisted living facility. Where she would be with other people her own age, and have friends to talk to. Somewhere she would not be alone and she wouldn't have to cook.

(*OK, he is saying all of the right things. Maybe this will work out all right.)*

I spoke with Shawn at the mortgage company. As it turns out, they are 8 months behind and I am trying to find out just what it would take for reinstatement. I learned that the house was in foreclosure with no sale pending yet. If we could come up with 6 payments in 48 hours it would put them at a 90 day delinquency. I learned also that a letter of First Intent to Foreclose had been sent to Mom and Jim on April 12, 2009, which had been ignored. In reality, Mom had put it in her desk, never gave it another thought and Jim never saw it.

So many emotions and thoughts were going through my mind.

(*This could be a blessing in disguise. It could be the catalyst that is needed to get Mom out of the house. What would Jim do? Where would he go? What happens when a house goes into foreclosure? Since the house is in Jim's name, it really isn't my concern, right? My responsibility is to get my Mom in a secure safe place to live and to get the important furniture and memorabilia out of the house before the locks are put on the door.*"

We had been doing some casual, preliminary research into assisted living facilities, now it looked like we had run out of time and options. This could be a good thing, after all. Move Mom into assisted living, where she would be safe and have help with meals and meds, but still have her own apartment and her own furniture. Let the house go into foreclosure, because I know there is no way that Jim can afford it on his own. He could then get his own small apartment, or move in with the girlfriend. All my problems solved!

Jim's girlfriend was at the house helping him to go through his files and trying to find some money, somewhere, that could help him get this mess straightened out. She had the nerve to call me and ask if I could loan him the money!

(Seriously???? With all that I was already doing to take control of this situation and straighten out this mess!! She could not tell me that she had been witnessing our Mother showing obvious signs of dementia, and she was a nurse! She knew more than I did what she was seeing, she could have been a big help from the very beginning, and now she thinks she has the right to ask me to loan my brother 6 months of house payments! That answer would be, NO!)

The two of them did enough digging around in his file cabinet and found a couple of CDs through a former employer that he could cash in and it would be enough to pay up the mortgage payments.

Now, even more angry feelings are bubbling up to the surface. My blood is boiling! My Mother, living on Social Security and a small retirement check, had taken out a second mortgage on the house to help Jim pay on his severely over extended credit card debt.

Yet, he has the money sitting in his own file cabinet and he could have taken care of his own debt, but instead he had let Mom come to his rescue, once again. Mom had quite literally put herself into the poorhouse in order to protect her son, and now, I am delegated to straighten out the mess! An honest effort on his part to find a job would have helped here too!

Mom must, on some level realize what is happening, and that she will be losing her home. She has been very co-operative in getting important pieces of furniture out of the house and into storage. I have stressed repeatedly that the bank could be putting locks on the doors any day now. We have moved out the corner china hutch; her sewing cabinet; the cedar chest full of lifelong treasures, that she has had since she was a teenager, and her roll top desk. I have told her that we are putting them in storage where they will be safe. At a later date, I will take the time to go through it all and see what is stashed away in all of the drawers and cubby holes.

For many months, Mom and I had watched a building going up on a road that we traveled often going to and from her doctor visits. Turned out to be an assisted living facility and they accepted state assistance. It was an answer to my prayers, to find something that we could afford and so close to home, only 2 miles from my driveway to their parking lot. Now, I would just have to try to convince Mom to check it out. Once again God was watching out for me.

Dan and I told Mom that we were going to check out the new place and then go out to dinner. She was receptive to the idea, but also let it be known that there was no way that she could afford to live in that nice new building. It had to be very expensive.

We pulled into the parking lot and the first thing we noticed were several elderly men and women sitting outside on nice little park benches. I said, "Look Mom, you will be able to make some new friends, maybe even find a boyfriend." She quickly responded with, "I don't NEED a boyfriend and I don't WANT one either! I DON'T KNOW WHY WE ARE EVEN HERE!" Great, I had just put her in a bad mood; this was not going to go well. We walked inside and saw the warmth and home like feeling. From the fireplace and nice couches placed for easy conversation, with a piano near the elevators. One of the elderly ladies came over to Mom and took her hand and started talking to her right away and asked if she was moving in. Mom told her, "Maybe, we are here to look around." The other lady assured her that she would like it here, that it was a very nice place.

We took the tour, and saw the library room; the activity area; the exercise room; the dining room; the nice, large sized, individual apartments with big bathrooms and even bigger walk-in closets. Mom was very impressed and said she would enjoy living there, if she could afford it. The woman giving us the tour assured her that she would be able to afford it.

When we returned downstairs at the conclusion of the tour, the elderly resident was still near the fireplace. She immediately came over and inquired how Mom liked the place and would she be moving in? She told her name and said that she was from Chicago, and that if Mom moved in they could be friends.

(Okay God, that was a very nice touch you added here with that Chicago reference, you really helped to seal the deal with that one! Thank You!)

We went back the next day and filled out the paperwork and were now on a waiting list, which could take a couple of months. Mom was excited about her nice, new apartment, at least for now.

I have just learned that Jim was now working two jobs for the same temp service. He is in St. Louis during the day and then straight to his evening job of cleaning an office in a bank building not far from home. This had been going on for about a week before I was made aware of the fact that Mom was home alone all day and now all evening too. I can't help but be quite aggravated that Jim could not take the responsibility to let me know of the new change in their routine and just how much time Mom would be alone. *(Again, it shows just how disconnected from reality he is.)*

I received a phone call around 6:00 one evening; Mom was very upset that something had happened to Jim, something was very wrong. He didn't come home for supper. I tried to reassure her he was fine and that he was at work. She could not accept it; she just knew that something had happened to him. Dan went with me to Mom's house, to try and reassure her that Jim was alright. We told her we would go to where he worked and make sure that he was there. Now, I had no idea what building he worked in among the complex of offices and banks, but we drove around until I found his truck in the parking lot. I tried to call his cell phone, but it is either turned off or can't be heard over the vacuum cleaners and floor scrubbers. I left a message about how upset Mom was. I also left a handwritten note on the windshield of his truck, asking if the least he could do between jobs would be to give his Mother a call and let her know that he was going on to another job. It was hard for her to remember for all of those hours that he had two jobs. We went back to the house and sat with her until she was calm enough and understood that Jim would be home in just a little while.

Jim never called me back or responded in any way to the note that I had left on his windshield.

Very late one evening I received a call from Mom; she was crying and extremely upset about something she had seen on the TV news. She proceeded to tell me that someone had destroyed all of the graves of the priests buried behind Holy Family Church in Cahokia. She said that they had knocked down all of the stones and dug up the graves, the bodies were scattered all over the grounds. It was just awful that not even the dead could be respected anymore!

(This was personally upsetting for her, because an uncle and a cousin of hers, both priests, are buried there.)

Now, I had just watched the news myself and I did not hear about any such thing, so I changed the subject, calmed her down and talked until I knew that she was alright. I then called a former neighbor of ours who still lived on our old street, to see if she could validate the story. She could not. I then turned to the internet, scouring every local news source and turned up nothing. Something of this magnitude would certainly have been breaking news, but I found nothing.

The next morning, I called Mom to see how she was doing; this story was the first thing that she brought up. "How could someone destroy graves like that?" After a few minutes of conversation, I asked if she would like to go to Cahokia and see for herself how bad the damage was and we could go to lunch at Oliver's at the airport. She quickly responded with, "Oh yes, I would like that, I will get ready.

At Oliver's, as usual, we sat by the window and watched the planes land and take off, wondering who was coming and going.

After lunch, we drove over to Holy Family church; I parked the car in the parking lot and we walked around to the back of the church. There was the perfectly manicured lawn; undisturbed graves, the perfectly undamaged, marble cross monuments for each priest buried there. There were even silk flowers on our family member's graves. I gave her a few minutes to process the sight. She turned and looked at me and said, "WOW! Someone did a very good job at fixing it all up again! You can't even tell that they had been dug up, and look at the markers, they are perfect! I wonder who put flowers on Uncle Will's and Al's graves. We don't have much family left, who would do that."

Quickly thinking, I said, "Probably someone from the church does that, or maybe your cousin Sandy did it." She was okay with that answer and then she was ready to leave. We then walked back around front and over to the brick walkway to look for Grandma's commemorative brick that Mom had purchased when Grandma had died. We found it and she fussed like she has always done; that they didn't do it right, that she had not gotten the year that she had requested. It wasn't at all what she had asked for.

From there, we went to visit our former neighbors, the Smith's, so we could tell them the good news, that the damaged graves had been repaired.

I tried to call Mom around 5:00 pm and didn't get an answer. I left a message, knowing full well that she would not listen to it. She had forgotten a long time ago what that little black box with the flashing red light was for, or even how to use it. I waited about 20 minutes and called again, thinking that she could have been in the bathroom, or out in the back yard looking at her flowers, or outside talking to the neighbor; still no answer. When I called for the third time with no answer, I decided I had to go over and find out why she was not answering the phone. Of course, Dan would not let me go alone. We arrived just after 6:00 p.m., the house was dark and the TV was not on. I called out to her, with no answer; with fear mounting, and my heart pounding, I headed to her bedroom. She was snuggled in bed, the covers pulled up to her chin, sound asleep. I woke her up to make sure that she was okay. I asked her why she was asleep so early. Barely awake, she told me that she was so tired. She and Richard had gone to church that evening for a special Mass; it was very nice, but it was so long and she was tired. As soon as Richard brought her home, she went to bed.

(*I know that Richard had not been there, but HAD she wandered around somewhere by herself, or did she just imagine that she had went to church? Why was she so tired?*)

Another late evening phone call, with Mom crying hard and so upset that she could barely speak. I finally calmed her down enough so I could understand what she was trying to say. She said, "My cousin Linda just called to tell me that her Mother had died. My Aunt Fannie Mae died and Uncle Willie is so upset he doesn't know what he will do without her. He doesn't want to live now, either." I was speechless; while I was not prepared for this phone call, I was not totally surprised either. Several months earlier, I had been told by a friend of a very similar call from her Mother also going through Alzheimer's.

(*My mind was racing, trying to quickly figure out what was the right thing to say. I didn't want to upset her further, I also did not want to make light of the thoughts that were very real to her. No matter what I would say, I was sure I would upset her on some level. I didn't see any way to avoid it completely. Her aunt and uncle had both been dead for over 10 years. As my friend's story ran through my mind and how upset her Mother was, I am listening to my own Mom sobbing over the loss of her aunt.)*

I finally took a deep breath and said, "Mom, I know this really hurts and it is very sad news, but everything will be alright." She slowed her crying and then her mood changed slightly; I heard a deep breath on the other end of the phone, then, out- of- the blue, the question that I was not prepared for. **"Did you already know about this? Who told you? Why do you think you always have to be the first to know everything!"**

(Here I was, over my head into the conversation I had wanted to avoid. I felt like I was sinking in quicksand, I couldn't breathe, I knew there was a storm brewing and I didn't know how to stop it).

I said, "Mom, you called and told me yourself." Hoping that would be enough to satisfy her and to defuse her anger. She started yelling, **"I couldn't have told you, I just found out myself!"**

(I cringed as I continued on, knowing that there was no turning back at this point.)

"Mom, I know you are very upset, and it has been a long time since you have seen Aunt Fannie Mae. I guess you have forgotten that she died over 10 years ago." She now screamed, violently, **"You don't know what the hell you are talking about!"** She hung up on me. We never spoke of this conversation again.

I had also become concerned about whether or not Mom was eating properly, or even at all. I already knew that her medication was not being taken as directed, and with Jim living in his own little world, I was pretty certain he was not making sure that she was eating.

One afternoon, I made it a point to be at their house, well before Jim would leave for work, so I could see firsthand what they did for supper. Mom and I sat around in the living room talking for a while. Jim came out of his room, packed his lunch to take to work, told us good-bye and headed for the door. I asked about supper. Jim said his lunch that he was taking was his supper. After Jim walked out the door, I looked at Mom at Mom and asked about her supper. She said she was fine; she would have a snack later, because Jim had cooked them a big lunch earlier. She was not hungry now. I looked around and did not see any sign of cooking or dirty dishes. After a little while, I invited her to go out with me to eat. She wasted no time in getting her purse and off we went.

The next day, I made it a point to be at their house early enough to see this big lunch that Jim would supposedly make for them. Again, Mom and I were in her living room talking and watching TV. Shortly after noon, Jim came out of his room, made himself a couple of peanut butter sandwiches, grabbed some chips, and went back to his bedroom. He did not offer to fix her anything, or even ask if she wanted something. I then asked her about lunch; she said she had slept late and had really just had her breakfast. I was now getting a very clear picture of what was happening, or, what was not. Jim seeing to it that o u r Mother was eating was something that was just **not** happening.

From that day on, I would bring over stew, spaghetti, or meatloaf, saying I had made too much. Some days, I would pick up fast food and say that I was in the neighborhood and just wanted to stop by.

(I sure wish that the assisted living facility would call soon!)

Just a few days later I got a call from the assisted living facility. While they still did not have any openings at this location, there was availability at another location in the next town and that if we wanted to move into there for now and then when something opened up here, we could always change if we wanted to. Without hesitation, I said that we would take it and that yes, she could move in this weekend. I was not letting this chance slip by. I didn't care if I had to drive a little bit farther. I also did not take the time to consult with Mom or anyone else about going to the other location. I had to get Mom out of that house and under supervision. She simply could not be left alone any longer.

The paperwork was completed and Mom had been approved for state funded assistance. Combining the state funding with her social security, the retirement from Bridal Originals, and the insurance draws; her rent was covered and she would be left with $30.00 a month for personal expenses.

OCTOBER 2009

MOVING IN TO ASSISTED LIVING

7

THE MOVE TO ASSISTED LIVING

October 2009

When moving day arrived, I had insisted that everyone had to help, that Mom was not going to think that I was the only one moving her. I needed both my brother and sister there to physically help as well as be supportive of this change in Mom's life. Of course, neither Jim nor Mom, had planned ahead and had not packed anything at all. I had expected as much and came prepared with boxes and packing materials. I had Linda take Mom to her bedroom and start packing up things that she would need in her new apartment. I put Jim in the kitchen and told him to pack up two plates, two cups, two of each fork, knife and spoon, etc. In the apartment, Mom would have a microwave, but no stove, so she would not need any pots and pans. I delegated Dan and Ray to start moving out the furniture. Mom's bookcase, her rocking chair, and side table and the bakers rack for her kitchenette. I packed books, pictures and nick-knacks. In a couple of hours we were finished packing, trucks and vans all loaded we were ready to go. When suddenly, Mom asked, "Where are we going? What are we doing?"

Linda said that while she and Mom had been packing up her bedroom, Mom was telling her all about her nice new apartment and what a big closet it had. Now she wondered what we were doing.

We had two vans and two pickup trucks loaded when we arrived at the assisted living complex. While we were unpacking and setting the furniture in place, Mom looked around the room, kind of puzzled. She looked at Jim and asked, "Where is your bed going to go?" He said, "I can't stay here, I am not old enough." Of course she wanted to know where he was going and what he would do. He told her was going to go live with his girlfriend, so that made it okay. All in all, the move went smoothly and she accepted that it was the way it was going to be.

On Monday I took her shopping to get some new things for her apartment. We bought a bright flowered shower curtain and coordinating bath mats, a shoe rack, laundry basket and several other odds and ends.   She was very happy and proud of all of her new things.

Mom was quite happy with her new apartment; she told everyone that Mearl had found this place for her. He made sure that she was in a good place. He had taken care of her as a child and he was taking care of her now. I was so relieved that she was happy with those thoughts. I could only hope that on days when she would be disgruntled and mad, she would also be sure to blame him and not me! I was still quite grateful for his suggesting to her to make the move into assisted living. It had made my life easier.

About a week later, we went to Walgreens to get a few things; it was as if she had never been in a store before. She walked around in amazement of how big this place was. She picked up everything that she could get her hands on, she had to look and touch everything. She read dog and cat food labels, proclaiming that this store had "Everything!" When we added a box of tissues to our cart, she said, "I can't believe how one store can have everything in it. It is going to take us all day to get through this place." I knew that the days of going shopping to someplace as large as Wal-Mart were over for us. It would be very mind boggling for her to be in such a large place.

The assisted living complex provided many opportunities for going out to the library, various eating places, Wal-Mart, and even the casino, but Mom never wanted to participate in those activities. I personally think she was afraid of getting lost or left behind, though she would never admit that.

Now that Mom was safe and enjoying her new life with friends her own age, I could concentrate on going through all of the boxes of papers that we had taken out of her desk. I needed to sort through it all and try to make sense of what had been shoved in the drawers.

I discovered that she had bought and sold insurance policies over the years, almost like a day trader. Bought, sold, canceled and bought again through another company. Many of the policies that I came across, I could not tell if they were valid or not. I spent many hours and days making phone calls and faxing POA papers to each one before they would confirm or deny the policies.

I found one life policy that appeared to be quite new, as well as the card for the salesman. It turns out that he had sold Mom numerous policies over the years. We discussed this most recent policy, he was surprised to learn that Mom had been diagnosed with dementia and was taking Aricept®. She had not told him this information when she was filling out the application. He also stated that she did not appear to be confused about anything during their interview process. With this new information that I had given him, he said the policy would be voided, because Mom had not been truthful on the application when asked about medical exams and drugs.

Later, I found another policy that appeared to be in effect. I eventually learned, after many phone calls and faxes, that indeed it was still in force and was told the cash value. Now what do I do with this information, knowing that with Mom on state aid, she could not have the money. I called the state and told them of my discovery. Per their instructions, I cancelled the policy and requested the cash value. This was deposited into our joint bank account. I then contacted our local funeral home and planned a pre-paid funeral. We could not keep the actual life policy in effect as it had cash value to Mom and/or her family. But, by paying in advance to the funeral home, we could not benefit from it. The policy was not enough to cover the most simple

Funeral. I paid what I could and would have to personally make payments out of my own pocket for the balance due, but that is the way it would have to be. The funeral is planned; and it is a good feeling to know that those major decisions are made and I will not have to deal with them later.

Mom enjoyed roaming the halls in the early evening hours and visiting with the women sitting around in the various little lounge areas. Some crocheted while they visited, others just chatted. Sometimes those early evening social hours turned into very late night gatherings. It was almost like a huge slumber party for senior citizens.

Usually, whenever I went for a visit, I would find Mom sitting in her chair doing some kind of hand stitching, usually on a quilt that she had been working on for several years.

Mom had been a seamstress for most of her adult life. She had made many of her own clothes and then clothes and pajamas for her children. She earned extra money by making clothes for other family members and friends. Eventually, she became a seamstress making wedding dresses for Bridal Originals.

On one of my visits she was hemming a pair of her slacks. Slacks that she had owned for a long time, but now had decided that they were way too long. She was also wearing a pair of newly hemmed slacks. She stood to show me how much better they fit. I could barely control the laughing! At first I thought they were inside out, but a closer look revealed that they were on right, but the hem was on the outside of the pant and it was folded almost up to her knee! Let's just say she was creating her own fashion statement, while turning all of her slacks into cropped pants!

Whenever Mom was sitting in her chair sewing, she liked to prop the door open so she could watch people walking up and down the hallway. I think it was partly so she could easily invite people in to visit with her. She would tell me how the various people had admired her sewing skills.

Almost a year later I found paperwork that indicated the possibility of another life policy. I called and inquired, again sent proof of POA and eventually learned that yes, indeed it was a valid policy, payable upon death. However, the company was in receivership and could not pay out any cash value money. They could only pay upon death. They were attempting to sell the company and would let me know when that happened and when I could request a cash payout. There was nothing more that I could do regarding this policy, except file the policy away and wait.

8

THE EVENTS OF 2010

It didn't take Mom very long after moving into assisted living to develop the paranoia that people were stealing from her. She was always saying what a great place she had, with all the good food, and the fun things to do. She said she had good friends to talk to and to eat with, she was very happy at not having to cook and wash dishes, but was frequently annoyed at how people would break into her room and steal things.

On my visits when she would start in about something new being missing and that she had to always hide things so no one could find her stuff, I would ask her where she hid it. Of course she did not know where she hid that particular item. So I would offer to look for it for her. I always asked permission to look in her dresser drawers or under her bed. I had to show her that I still respected her privacy and that I would not go snooping around without her permission. Every time I found the missing item, she proclaimed that it was not in the place where she had hid it. Someone had moved it.

Mom began to write notes asking that who ever stole her ring, (or money, or hearing aids) to please return them. They did not belong to them and she wanted the items back. She asked that whoever stole the item to please just slide it under the door. The note was then attached to her door for everyone to see. She used the postage stamps that I had left in her desk, as the stickers to hold the note to the door!

One day in particular when I arrived for a visit, she was in a downright ugly mood. She was talking so mean and blaming the cleaning people who come into her room all the time. Like talking to a child, I tried to make her see that she was not being very nice, that these were very nice people and they wouldn't steal from her. They would lose their jobs.

Mom got up from her chair, and in the voice and antics of a toddler, she started waving her arms, and ranting that she was a 2 year old, and not a very nice girl. She stomped over to her bed and flopped down sitting on the edge with her feet dangling and not reaching the floor, she swung them back and forth while singing, "I'm a little 2 year old and you don't like it, NA- NA- Na. I'm a little 2 year old and you don't like it, NA-NA-NA". I had to turn around and walk back to the living room so I could openly laugh. It was the funniest sight ever! I didn't dare let her see me laughing so hysterically!

After a few verses of her singing, she quit, and

came back into the living room. The mood was over and all was fine. She sat down and talked like there had never been a problem. Just as with a child, she got over it much quicker, since I ignored her behavior, then she would have if I had confronted the situation.

When Mom was in her childish mood and being the naughty little girl that she could be, she quite often would stick her tongue out at me. She also liked to flip her tongue back and forth across her lip and sass with "blah, blah, blah…… BLAH!"

(There was always that last louder, firmer "blah" for emphasis! What would she have done to me, if I had acted like this when I was a child?)

March 3, 2010

Today is my birthday and I want to celebrate it with my Mother. We went to get haircuts and then out to lunch at Denny's. She got her favorite meal of chicken strips and then we shared a hot fudge sundae. On the ride back to her apartment, she started singing, "You are my sunshine, my only sunshine." I joined in with her; she looked at me with bright eyes and a big smile and said, "You know this song?" We sang all the way back to her apartment. Maybe I was reading more into it than what was really there, but I believe this was truly a gift from above. Mom's communication skills had deteriorated greatly and I took it as her way of saying, I love you. Although, saying I love you, was not something that Mom had ever said much at all in my lifetime. I think that is what made this song even more special. (Especially, as time went on during the next couple of years, she sang, "You are my sunshine, my only sunshine," everytime I was with her. I claimed claimed it as "our song." It was her way of saying, "I love you.")

I had often read and heard that when working with an Alzheimer's person, it is very much like being with a two year old child. I had an "ah-ha" moment one day as we were leaving the doctor's office. Mom has never been one to hold hands or to walk arm in arm as so many mothers and daughters do. Even now, she resists an offered hand. She does not walk beside me, she follows. As we walked across the parking lot, I had a sense of being a Momma duck with my duckling following right behind. I chuckled, as she followed me completely to the driver's door. At one time it would have been obvious for her to go to the passenger side, but not anymore. I had to lead the way to the other side. I learned from then on that I was the leader and that she would follow, but we could not walk together.

On another visit to the doctor, Mom's childlike personality came out in full display for him. It started with him questioning her about getting a flu shot. Mom told him that she already had gotten one at her apartment that very day. I interjected that she had put her name on a sign-up sheet to get a flu shot the following week, but had not gotten the shot yet. She gave me a glaring look and started swinging her legs and singing, 'Yeah, that's right, I'm a 2 year old, and I don't know anything." She quit the childlike singing, looked at me and yelled, "I know I had a shot, you weren't there, you don't know everything!" The doctor looked at me, and said, "I don't think I have to tell you what time it is getting to be. You know what you need to start doing. He turned his attention to Mom, "Virginia, how have you been eating? How is your appetite? Are you sleeping well?" Mom returned to herself and answered his questions direct and politely. In his examination, he looked at both of her arms where she should have gotten a shot and saw no needle marks. He shook his head and simply said, "No."

The following week, on the day that the visiting nurses were at the assisted living facility, I received a phone call saying that Mom was refusing to get her shot. She was insisting that she had gotten a shot last week at her doctor's office. They wanted me to come to try and talk her into getting the shot.

When I arrived, I was informed that I could get a shot too, so I hoped to use that as my leverage for getting her to agree to get one as well. At first she agreed, but before we could get it done, her mood changed and she started yelling loudly that she had already had it done at her doctor's office. I looked her square in the eye and said, "No, you did not, you told the doctor that you didn't need one, because you already had gotten one, but you didn't. Today is the day to get it done, and see I am getting one too." I went first and then said, "Now it is your turn." She stuck her tongue out at me, as she stepped forward to let the nurse give her the shot. When it was over, she retorted, "There, are you happy now?" and stuck her tongue out at me once again.

(A sigh of relief covered up the laughing I was trying to hold back.)

November 14, 2010

Some days get to me more than others. Some days I walk away from visiting Mom feeling good. Some days I feel bewildered and helpless. And then there are days I am so upset, I don't know who to be mad at, who I really need to yell at, who I wish I could hit and get "it" out of my system. Whatever "it" is; I don't know. Someone needs to help me understand what these feelings are. Today, I can't really describe these feelings, not one single word to truly define them, the best word would probably be "lost."

I went to Mass at my church and sang in the choir, as usual. Then I drove through McDonalds to grab a breakfast sandwich and sweet tea, something to hold me over, until after I take Mom to her Mass at Holy Trinity. When I arrived at the Assisted Living complex, Mom was sitting at her usual seat in the dining room with her friends. Mom was telling her story about how Frank Sinatra used to come to her house in Chicago for lunch whenever he was in town performing. According to her, Frank was a frequent guest at their house.

(I had never heard this before and according to her brother it never

happened. However, this tale was becoming one told quite frequently.)

Mom was glad to see me, but also surprised. She said she was waiting for Jim to come and take her to church. I told her today was my turn to take her to church. Then she started with her excuses. She didn't want to make me go all the way over there; it wasn't necessary for me to go to church again, since I had already been to my own. I kept trying to reassure her that it was okay and that I didn't mind going to church again. Then she said we didn't need to go out to church, there is church right here. She invited me to go upstairs to attend Mass with her. So okay, we went upstairs.

(She had told me several times about going to Mass there with the woman priest, and her kids. So I was not sure what to expect. Was it really a Catholic Mass, or a non- denominational service? Either way, I was about to find out.)

We went upstairs to the library room. There was a table set up in the middle of the room with a stack of Missals on one side; in the center of the table was a freestanding table top crucifix; a crystal bowl of Holy Water at the front right hand corner. A young woman wearing a pretty pink sweater was standing at the head of the table making notes in a journal book. As we walked in the door, she turned to Mom, and warmly said,

"Hello, Virginia, so glad to see that are you joining us today. It is good to see you." And then, I noticed that she picked up a sheet of paper that had a list of names on it and she checked off Mom's name. So, it was obvious that Mom had been there before. I learned the lady in the pink sweater was a Eucharistic Minister from the nearby Catholic Church and she holds a Communion Service for the residents. There was a tape player sitting on the floor behind the lady's husband and her two nieces, who had come to help her with the service. Traditional Catholic hymns filled the room as we waited for everyone to arrive.

It was interesting to see these people in this near church-like setting and how their demeanors were quite different from what I normally see in the dining room. One woman was singing along quite loudly with each song. She knew every word to every song, and was quite clearly enjoying the moment. Another woman became a real mystery to me. I have seen this woman almost every time I visit Mom. I know she is deaf and she always has a big smile for me. She does sign language and always points out my lipstick and my eyes. If I am wearing a red top, she points to my lips and then to my shirt. She mouths the word "pretty" along with the sign for pretty, and says in a broken voice "ma-a-a-a-tch," as she points back and forth between the shirt and my lips. Now, she sits waiting for Mass to start; she begins giving dirty looks to the woman who is loudly singing, she starts shaking her head, "no," and with her fingers to her mouth motions for her to, "zip her lip!" She looks my way, shakes her head and rolls her eyes. Again she motions to "zip it!" Can she really hear her? I am smiling with delight and amusement at her perception of what is taking place.

Then, there is the tall thin man who is always a very loud constant talker. Usually wearing just a white, sleeveless, cotton tee shirt; today he is dressed in a nice, striped shirt, sitting on the couch, being very quiet and prayerful. Eventually, there are twelve people gathered or accounted for and the lady in the pink sweater begins her service.

While I "know" all of the people sitting in this room, they have each taken on a different persona, here in this somewhat reverent setting. They are like totally different people from who I normally see on a day to day basis.

When Mass was over, I offered to take Mom out to eat at IHOP, but first we went to her room to make a potty stop before heading out. I was looking at the books in her bookcase, when she came out of the bathroom. She came over and pointed to the wedding picture of her and Dad, she said, "See the picture of me with my boyfriend, Richard." I said, "This is not Richard, this is Dad." She looked at me then looked at the picture again. She said, "Where is Richard's picture?" She started rummaging through the other bookshelves, looking for Richard's picture, asking over and over again, "Where is Richard's picture?"

At IHOP, Mom ordered banana bread french toast; she cut the french toast with the knife and then continued to use the knife like a fork for the first few bites. I gently suggested that she use the fork, it will be easier. She said "OK" and picked up the fork and proceeded to eat.

(So why did today bother me so much? Was it seeing the simple beauty of God's work within the lost

minds of these people, who on some level, knew that they were at church and they knew how to act and behave? Was it from Mom's deep confusion over Richard and Dad? I thought I had already understood where her mind was with that situation. Was it realizing that she cannot figure out to switch utensils into her other hand in order to eat, instead of using just whatever is in her left hand at the moment when she chooses to take a bite. Was it realizing that she is slipping farther away and there is nothing that I can do about it, except pray!)

Knowing that the day would be coming when Mom would have to leave assisted living and be in a more secure facility, I started doing my research again. I set about visiting different nursing facilities and like before, I felt like Goldilocks looking for the right bed. This one was too old and out-dated, I didn't like the smell of that one. In another, the residents all looked like spaced out zombies with no life in them at all.

The most important factors that I had to use to make my decision revolved around making sure that the place was secure, she could not escape and they had to accept state aid. I soon learned those two things do not go hand in hand very often. Most nursing homes would accept state aid, but not in their secure Alzheimer's Unit. I could put her in the nursing home side with the help of the state, but if she walked away, how could I live with that? I had read and heard too many horror stories of dementia patients walking away and being found miles away, and not always alive. I could not take a chance on my Mom's well-being. I had to keep looking.

My options narrowed down to two, neither of them in my county. One was 20 miles south of us in Monroe County, with a good reputation and of course a waiting list of probably a couple of months. My reservations about it, was that it seemed so remote, out in the middle of a corn field, and no local hospital in case of an emergency.

My other option was 20 miles north in Madison County, just 2 miles off the Interstate, with a hospital right across the street. A totally new state of the art facility, but the problem here being that it was still under construction and it already had a waiting list as well. Safe and secure dementia units are in high demand and will become increasingly more so.

Weighing the pros and cons of the two places, of course the nice, new facility would be ideal; only two miles off the interstate would mean easy access for my sister and her grown children with their little ones, who are back and forth on that highway all the time for various reasons. Mom would certainly enjoy random visits from grandkids and great grandkids. They could easily pop in and out for a short visit with Grandma, without going out of their way. There were also a couple of hotels and restaurants very close by for any out of town relatives who might choose to visit. This location would also be more convenient for Jim to make visits as well. Mom would certainly have the opportunity for more visitors with this location.

Now, I would just have to wait and see who would call first. It was a real gamble during this waiting period; Mom's dementia was progressing, and that at any time assisted living could say that it was time for her leave. I made it a point to keep their office aware of my search and the waiting lists that we were on. Somehow, I thought that as long as I kept them informed they would work with me.

Then, out of the blue a week later the nursing home out in the cornfield, with the months long waiting list called and said that they had an opening. I wasn't expecting this so quickly. Mom didn't need to move right now, but soon. I really wanted to wait for the new place near the highway. My head was hurting from trying to juggle all of the *what-if's*. Do I move her out to the middle of corn field with nothing around and knowing no one would drive that far to see her except me? Do I pass on this and wait for the new place and hope that Mom gets in and that they accept her? Will Mom be alright in assisted living until the new place is ready? What if she doesn't get in, what if she has to move out of assisted living and I have passed up the chance at the first place? No one could help me with this decision. I was completely on my own.

I chose to hold off for the new facility near the hospital and the interstate. It was the only way that Mom would possibly have any visitors besides me.

(I prayed hard that I was making the right decision on this.)

9

THE EVENTS OF 2011

January 24, 2011

I had been sick for a couple of weeks and unable to go visit and see for myself how Mom was doing. She was happy and surprised to see me. She knew Dan and called him by name. She had not done that for a while. Mom asked how I was and also what we were doing out. She asked if we were going shopping. I told her that I had been sick and at the doctors and was taking medicine. She said, "OK" and then went on to tell a strange story about Jim and how she sees him every day. He is working on the roads and bridges right outside the building and he eats lunch with her every day. *(He does not.)* She said the people here make sure that he is well taken care of. She went on to talk about her friend Richard. She asked again what we were doing, and were we going shopping? She asked Dan how he was. Then again, she tells another story about Jim working on the roads and how dangerous it is. She asked if Dan and I were going shopping. Then again, she talked about Richard. I told her I had just adopted two dogs.

She asked if Dan and I were going shopping. In between each of these repeated conversations she talked to her lady friends, that dinner should be coming soon. It was quite clear that she was not absorbing any part of my conversation with her, so when their dinner plates arrived I told her we were going shopping and Dan and I left.

Feb. 12, 2011

I had just gotten a haircut and was heading to the apartment to visit with Mom, when I got a phone call from the Director of Nursing. She said that Mom was standing in the hallway outside her room with the door open, barefooted, appearing to be intently talking to someone who was not there. The nurse also went on to say that she had tried to talk to Mom and to get her attention, but she could not reach her. She thought I should come see for myself. I was already pulling into the parking lot. When I got upstairs, Mom was now sitting on her bed, attempting to put on her shoes and socks, still deeply conversing with whomever it was that she was mentally with. She was saying, "Yes, that's right, right, that's right. No, it is M-A-N-R-I- N-G. "Yes," "No,"
"M-A-N-R-I-N-G." "Right, right, yes, that's it. Oh that is good, yep, yep" and then she laughed out loud. "Yes,

I know, - - it was Al Capone, - - yes he was here, - - I saw him." The nurse looked at me with surprise and said, "What? Why is she talking about Al Capone?" She walked over to face Mom who was still bent over putting on her shoes. The nurse tried to get her attention again, and this time she got through the delusion that Mom was in. Mom looked up at her in total confusion. The nurse asked her who she was talking to, and Mom said, "You." The nurse said, "No, just a minute ago you were talking to someone else about Al Capone, who were you talking to?" Mom smiled and said, "Oh, those nice young men, they work at Scott Air Force Base and they wanted to know my name and all about me. We were having a good talk, they were so nice and they live across the hall, right over there," as she pointed towards the door. "They are good hard working boys." The nurse asked again about Al Capone, but Mom had tuned her out again and was concentrating on her shoe. So, I filled the nurse in on the fact that Mom grew up on the south side of Chicago. The building that she lived in rented out rooms, and Mr. Capone himself, had been there to rent a room. So, talking of Al Capone was not completely a part of her imaginary world, he had been real.

(Adding to the events of this day, there were the numerous times that she had told me that Whitey Herzog lived across the street and how she always went over and talked to him whenever she saw him outside mowing his grass. Did she really go across the street and talk to some man cutting his grass? Did he look like Whitey Herzog? Or did she just simply watch someone from her window, and imagine that she had talked to him? I knew that the time had really come, that it was time for Mom to move on to a secure Alzheimer's Unit. Her days of living in an assisted living facility were over.)

Feb. 25, 2011

The complex celebrates birthdays on the last Friday of the month with cake and ice cream and some form of live entertainment. Today, I happened to arrive in the middle of the party. Mom was totally involved in her own little world. Singing and clapping along with the man playing the guitar. She was also so involved in her cake and ice cream; she was not aware that I was even there. I watched, as with each bite she took, she slowly and intently licked her spoon clean on both sides, as if she were eating a lollipop, before going back into the bowl for another scoop, then again licking the spoon like a lollipop. She didn't miss a drop.

Mon. Feb. 28, 2011

Today is the day for the assessments from the Alzheimer's Unit where Mom is expected to move to. Mom is not aware of this impending move. I am wondering what they are going to be telling her, as to who and why they are there? I would like some info ahead of time. Forgetting that they are the professionals and do this all the time, it is my lack of knowledge of what is about to take place that I fear. I realize that I am not in charge and have no control over these events. I am lost and in a state of confusion, very much like my own Mother. When I arrive at Mom's apartment, there are two ladies; one is the assessment person, the other lady is the director of the Memory Care Unit. Together, they will decide if Mom does indeed need the specialized care that they can offer. They will also decide if she will fit in with the other residents and staff. *(I later learned that sometimes a person with dementia who is extremely violent would need a different care unit).* The assessment person is bright, talkative and very intuitive. She tells Mom that she is a coworker of mine wanting to see her apartment and asks how she likes it at this place, because she is looking for an apartment for own Mom. The three of them talk of anything and everything; from sewing; the pictures on the bookcase; Mom's friend Richard; Mom's high school friend Eleanor; Mom even points out her wedding picture and calls Dad by the nickname of his youth, " Blackie." I cannot remember the last time I had ever heard Mom or anyone else call him that. (In his younger days he had a head full of thick dark black hair.) As they prepare to leave, the young director gives Mom a hug, then asks her, if she would like to come visit her house and have coffee with her and some friends. Mom smiles and says she would like that very much. I get a nod and the director says she will make the proper arrangements for Mom. After they leave, Mom tells me how nice those ladies were and that I have good friends. She went to the window to watch them get into their car and waved goodbye to them.

I literally felt a weight had been lifted from my shoulders. I could breathe again, for the first time in quite a while. It was comforting to know that Mom would be moving to a safe place and would get the constant 24 hour care that she truly needed. It was a nice, new state –of- the- art place, with a very friendly and caring staff, and easy access to the highway for other family visitors.

(I think I have everything taken care of that needs to be handled; now it is just a bit more paperwork and organize the actual move.)

I notified the assisted living facility that Mom has been accepted and that we are waiting for the paperwork process to get a move-in date. I am informed by the assisted living director to submit the notice in writing, and that since we are starting a new month, I would need to pay the full month's rent due for March since we did not have an actual moving date. She went on to tell me if we moved before the 15th of the month, we would get a refund of a half month's rent. If we did not move before the 15th, then we would pay the full month.

(I am also trying to figure out in my head, how I will pay a full month's rent here, as well as a months' rent at the new place too. Social Security and pension checks are not enough to cover both places! How is this going to work out? How much will I have to cover out of my own pocket?)

Oh, and one more thing, we would need to complete the move in one day. The keys would need to be turned in before the business office closed at 4:30 p.m.

(I wasn't sure just how I could accomplish getting Mom

(I wasn't sure just how I could accomlish getting Mom out and settled in her new place 20 miles away, as well as totally packing up everything she owned and moved out by 4:30 p.m. No stress with those instructions!! I can't solicit help at this point; I don't know when I will need the help. I must try to be patient. I hadn't come this far by myself and I knew that with enough prayer, God would get me through this hurdle, like He had so many times before. All I could do now was to wait, and pray!)

After a few days I am on pins and needles, the clock is ticking; we are well into our first week of March and no word from the Memory Care Unit. I can't go over to Mom's apartment and pre-pack anything; she doesn't know she is moving. All the doctors and nurses have advised that in her state it was best to not tell Mom about the move ahead of time; she would worry too much and become overly agitated. When moving day comes we would play it by ear, and together we would devise a plan. Continue to wait.

I am trying to be patient, but the waiting is eating away at me. After a few more days, I call to try to find out when we can move. It is during this conversation I learn that all new residents are moved into The Memory Care Unit on Mondays and only one resident per week;

and there was someone ahead of Mom on the list. *What???*

They explained, that this was done in order to allow the staff to give closer one-on-one attention to the new resident. It gives the resident a full week to settle into their new home, to get beyond the initial feelings of being lost and confused in their new surroundings. Their plan made sense, once it was explained to me, but why couldn't this have been told to me before now. It certainly would have saved me from a few panic attacks and sleepless nights.

Finally, I got word that Mom's move- in date is Monday, March 14th and she needs to be there around 9:30 a.m. I only have a couple of days to organize my plan for the day, and figure out how I am actually going to pull this off.

A few days before the scheduled move, while Mom was downstairs getting her hair done, I asked her for the key to her apartment, so I could go watch TV while she was getting pretty. I very quickly packed a suitcase with about two weeks worth of clothes, and stashed it in my van for taking to the Memory Care Unit on moving day. This would be enough for her to have on hand to start with. I then returned to the salon to wait for her to finish. Sadly, I watched a few of the other residents laughing and talking about Mom; who was sitting under the dryer, looking at a magazine and talking to the pictures, as if the pictures were talking back to her. She was holding quite the conversations with that magazine! While I thought it was rude of these ladies, I was very aware that Mom no longer belonged here. It truly was time to move on to the next level of care.

10
MOVING
TO THE MEMORY CARE UNIT

Monday March 14, 2011

On this very bitter, cold, gray day; a heavy, wet mix of sleet and snow was falling. A gloomy day to match the mood I was feeling.

Jim had arranged to have the day off to assist with getting Mom physically moved from one location to the other. I had hoped that having him there would ease her anxieties. Dan had also taken the day off. He was stationed at the far end of the Assisted Living parking lot in his pick-up truck with our flatbed trailer in tow. He was armed with packing boxes and supplies. He was positioned to be able to see whenever Jim and I left with Mom, so he could go in and start the packing of her dishes, books, nick-knacks and such. Jim and I were to join him, after getting Mom settled in her new home.

Mom was in the dining room, still eating her breakfast when Jim and I walked in. Imagine her surprise to see the two of us together so early in the morning. We told her to go ahead and finish her breakfast; we would wait over by the fireplace since we were cold. In the meantime, we met with the Director of Nursing and had decided that, with the weather as cold as it was, we would tell her that her furnace was not working properly; she could not stay there with no heat and that there were no extra rooms for her to stay in. She would be going to another location for a few days. She accepted the plan without question, and assisted in packing an overnight bag with the necessary items that she would need for a couple of days. She bundled up for the bitter cold and tied on her little nylon head scarf. We got in Jim's truck and drove away. Dan moved into position and began to pack.

As we drove the 20 miles in the heavy falling snow, I was quite grateful that Jim was driving! Mom was in a cheerful fun mood. She was laughing and talking. She said she wanted to go out and build a snowman when we got where we were going. She and Jim talked about some of the various snowmen that they had built over the years.

When we arrived, the Move - In Coordinator met us at the door and welcomed Mom, and said she had been waiting for her. She said she would show Mom her room where she would be staying. We made our way to the secure Memory Care Unit area, where we were handed off to the Director of the unit. At this time, the switch inside Mom's head flipped and she began yelling and screaming at all of us. Her arms were flailing in all directions. Jim backed up to keep from getting smacked in the face. She glared at me and said, "You never tell me anything! Just get the hell out of here."

The director put her arm around Mom and spoke softly to her, "Virginia, tell me what is bothering you, do you remember when I was at your home last week, and invited you to come see me? You said you would like to visit. I have a room ready for you, come with me." Mom calmed down and walked with the director to the room. The director showed Mom her bed and the beautiful armoire that would be her closet. She helped Mom remove her coat and hang it in the armoire. She showed her the huge bathroom and then the flat screen TV on the wall and gave her the remote control and showed her how to operate it.

Jim and I are told to go get the rest of Mom's things from the truck while she finished showing, Ms. Virginia, around. When we returned, Mom was sitting at a table with a couple of other ladies, drinking coffee, talking and appearing to be enjoying the new company.

We placed her clothes in her room and walked over to the table where she was sitting. When my very pleasant Mother looked at me, that switch flipped again and she was once again in a tirade! She started yelling very loudly, "Why don't you just get the hell out of here! You just are dumping me here, go away. **GO**! Get the hell out. Do what you want to do, but go!" The director was right there with her arm around my shoulders, turning me away from Mom's view. She said it was time for us to go; she assured me that Mom would be fine as soon as we left. She said, "This is just like when you left your babies at the babysitters and they cried while they could see you, and were fine, happy and playing once you are out of sight; she will be fine once you are gone." I was also told that it would be best if I did not visit for about a week. She needed time to adjust to her new home without being upset by my visits. I could call as often as I wanted and they would call with frequent updates, but visits needed to be held off for a while.

I turned back around to tell Mom goodbye. She was holding Jim's hand and telling him she loved him, and he was such a good son. She kissed his hand. As I tried to move in to tell her goodbye, she shooed me off, and said, "Get out of here!" I knew in my mind it was her fear of the unknown. I also knew I was doing the right thing for her well-being, but oh how my heart was breaking!

As we got to the front door, I was breaking down. The Move - In Coordinator was there waiting with open arms to hug me, she said that Mom would be fine, and that I would be too. I had known for two years that this day was coming; I had handled all the paperwork and had made all arrangements for Power of Attorney. I had taken care of insurance carriers, doctors, mortgage companies and numerous bill collectors. I thought I had everything under control, but I had not taken the time to make sure that when the paperwork was done, what would I do about me? I was not prepared for the sudden onslaught of guilt. I was certain in my heart that I had made the right decisions for both of us, all along the way. Y et the guilt was overbearing.

Jim and I headed back to the Assisted Living Facility to help Dan finish packing up the apartment there. We worked the rest of the day. We found her dentures that had been missing for weeks. They were under her bed, as were her hearing aids. She had become the collector of straws. There was a tube sock in her drawer that was stretched to capacity with straws.

I had noticed that whenever we went out to eat, Mom always put her straw in her purse, now I knew what she had done with them all. She had added to her growing straw collection. Every drawer had piles of used tissues. I don't think she ever threw away a used tissue. Tissues were also found in the pockets of every piece of clothing that had a pocket.

The wonderful caring staff would stop in and offer to get us anything we needed. They hauled out trash, as they saw the need, and when we were ready, someone was there to vacuum the carpet for us.

Finally, just minutes before the Business Office closed, I was able to turn in the keys and close the door to that chapter of our lives. We pulled away with two fully loaded pickup trucks and a flatbed trailer. In the graying, evening sky the heavy wet snow was turning more into sleet as we headed home. It had been a long and exhausting day. I was totally spent.

Various relatives and friends called to see how the day had went and to see how I was doing.

(I know that they meant well and thought that they were expressing their love and support. However, I was not ready to talk about my day to anyone. I needed to be alone in my thoughts. I was full of numerous emotions mixed with guilt. I was so overwhelmed with emotions

that I honestly could not have talked, even if I had wanted to.)

Tuesday March 15, 2011

The first thing in the morning, I called to see how the rest of the previous day and the night had been. The nurse on duty assured me that everything was fine; Mom had slept well and that she was now sitting at a table with the other ladies and eating a good breakfast.

Later that afternoon, I received a phone call from the head nurse, to give me the results of her initial examination and interview with Mom. She noticed Mom was not wearing any hearing aids or false teeth, nor were they listed on the check-in sheet. Mom had told the nurse that she never had any teeth, and she didn't need any hearing aids, because she was only 18 years old. She could hear just fine!

I informed the nurse that Mom had lost them several weeks ago, but that I had found both the teeth and the hearing aids under her bed yesterday while we were packing up the apartment. She said I could bring them up and just leave them at the nurse's desk.

This was going to be a long difficult week of not being able to go up and visit and see for myself how Mom was doing. Though, I did understand the reason behind their regulations of not visiting during the first week.

Their frequent phone calls with updates, kept me informed of Mom's progress, and eased my concerns during this difficult week.

MOTHER'S DAY 2012

11

GRANDMA'S QUILT

Shortly after my Grandma Wayne's death in 1994, Mom proceeded to work on an unfinished quilt that Grandma had apparently started many years earlier. The vintage fabrics brought back childhood memories of aprons that Grandma had made for raffling at the Annual Cahokia Volunteer Fireman's Picnic, dresses that she had made for herself and her granddaughters, and quilts that had been commissioned by various people that knew of her meticulous pride in her needlework. I was in awe of this quilt and expressed a great desire to own it one day. Not only did it flood me with childhood memories, but it was a unique pattern that I had never seen before. I did not know the name of the pattern, I had not seen it in any of my many quilting magazines, but I knew it had to be a variation of a "Nine Patch Block". The variation being that the four corner pieces have elongated tails, looking much like a kite, creating a curved opening under the middle square. An oval white piece of fabric fills this space and is the connector to the next block.

Mom, from the very beginning, let me know that she would be keeping the quilt; since it was the last one that Grandma had been working on. Then she scoffed at how poorly it was made, the squares were crooked and mismatched, and she was spending more time fixing and repairing than she was at completing.

Over the next several years, she would from time to time drag it out and work on it some more. Whenever I saw it, it never seemed to be much further along than it had been the last time. I never missed an opportunity to remind her that I would like to have it and she always let me know that she was keeping it. It stayed next to her chair, for her to easily pick up and do some hand stitching whenever she was in the mood.

When Mom moved into assisted living in the fall of 2009, the unfinished quilt went with her and took its rightful place in a basket next to her chair. During those first weeks of visits she was diligently stitching trying to get the quilt finished. Then one day the quilt was gone; I asked where it was, she did not know. She said she didn't know what I was talking about. I was heartbroken, and yet deep down, hoping that she had put it away and had forgotten about it.

On another visit I noticed that underneath her side table was a hunk of familiar looking fabric scraps. I picked it up and gasped at a chopped up narrow strip of fabric that was lying there on the floor, the backing cut off and the batting pulled out. I tried as calmly as I could to ask what had happened to the quilt. She replied, "It was too long, so I cut it off." I asked where the rest of it was, she did not know. But she still was not ready to give me even that small remaining scrap of my treasured quilt. I just hoped one day, I would be able to find the rest of it, or at least salvage what little bit that I knew remained.

Mom has just been moved out of assisted living and into Memory Care, here I am at home sitting in my recliner, my treasured quilt in my hands. Just as I had hoped, the heirloom was found in the bottom of a laundry basket in her closet. Smiling at the mess I have to straighten out! You see the quilt was actually in three pieces. Each piece has a few blocks that cannot be salvaged because they are so chopped and ragged. (*They may possibly be turned into a pillow top or some other memento.*) One section of the quilt was folded in half and seamed together to nearly form a pillowcase. The seam is overcast stitched probably ten different times. The white oval setting pieces are folded in half and stitched down with more heavy duty overcasting. The largest piece, that is pretty much in great shape, except for one end where the other pieces had been chopped away, it is very heavily quilted, but still has a LOT of quilting to be done in order to finish it. I just hope that my right hand can do justice to her itty bitty little left handed stitches! Then there is the edging that will need to be redone, all of the white ovals are folded inside and stitched down causing this big lumpy, bumpy ridge all around three sides.

I sit here with my seam ripper in hand trying to cut through numerous layers of overcast stitching, smiling at the memories that the vintage fabric scraps bring. Here I am, the third generation working on the same quilt as both my Mother and my Grandmother. (*And yes, scoffing at the mess that Mom has made of this quilt, just as she scoffed at Grandma's mess!!*)

I have to wonder, which one of my girls will take up where I leave off. Will she be smiling, and also scoffing at the mess that I will leave with her? Well, sweetie(s), just remember it is your legacy to continue stitching the generations together. Maybe, just maybe, I will be able to complete this multi-generational quilt and pass down a piece of history. A real treasured family heirloom.

Thank you, Grandma and Mom for teaching me to appreciate the beauty of what can be done with a small scrap of fabric and a needle and thread. Thank you, for sharing your talents and passing down the joy of creativity. Thank you also for teaching me to not give up hope. It is there as long as we keep looking for it.

Love you and miss you both!

Wednesday March, 23, 2011

I was finally given the okay to come visit. I was so pleased, to see a happy smiling woman, who proudly showed me around the place. The week of restricted visits presented me with a much different person than the one I had left the week before. She introduced me to some of her new friends. She showed me pictures on the wall that she liked. They were large nicely framed prints of old farmhouse porches, and fields. We looked at each one and she proclaimed how pretty it was.

We sat at a table and chatted. She informed me that this is a brand new building and that Mearl had built it. He had made sure that she had a good room here. He and his wife, Audrey, have that first room up there and they come to visit with her every day.

(There is a cute little couple that does have a room in the same wing, the small framed man has a little gray, bushy mustache,

but does not physically resemble Mearl at all. But I guess in Mom's mind, he does.)

Mom went on to say, what makes this place so perfect, is how close it is to California. She can go out that back door over there, walk over the hill and she can visit Tina and Harry anytime she wants to. She said it is so much fun, to walk over to their house and surprise them, as she is laughing with sheer joy at the thought of doing that. She said that they have cake and have a good time.

I am now even more certain that I have made the right decision to be sure that she is in a secure area that she cannot escape from. I could not have handled the thought of her wondering off somewhere and getting lost, and who knows what else could have happened. Of course, I know I will always wonder if I could have done more in the beginning to have helped her to stall or ward off this horrible disease. I will always wonder if I could have done more myself to see that she could have stayed at home longer. But in the end, I know that I have done all that I could to ensure her safety. She is well taken care of, she is well fed, and she is safe from harm. I can't ask for more.

March 28, 2011

My oldest daughter Tina and her husband Harry arrived from LA for a visit with Mom to see how she was doing. Though her spirits were upbeat and she talked and laughed with them, she did not really know who they were. Mom kept trying to share her snacks with Harry. Mom has always had a soft spot for Harry, ever since the first time she met him. He was from Chicago and that made him quite special in her book. Mom kept telling them that she goes out the back door to visit Tina and Harry. She went to visit them in their new house, and that California is out the back door. She also told Harry that she was very concerned about her house in Fairview Heights. She said that the house was being taken apart because of the highway coming through there. She asked Harry to make sure that we got all of her stuff out of the house, and she wondered where Jim would go. What would he do? Harry assured Mom that we would get everything out of the house and Jim would be alright.

Tina held her emotions in check until she stepped outside. It was not easy to see her Grandmother living in this fantasy world.

March 29, 2011

Our second day of visiting was more emotional and Tina had a harder time dealing with it. Mom was also more out of it and not involved with us. Mom had a glazed, lost look in her eyes for about the first 30 minutes. She was not present with us. It was difficult to hold a conversation. I think for the first time Tina actually began to realize what I have been dealing with.

April 18, 2011

Jim and I went together to celebrate Mom's birthday. We had presents and cards from family and friends. I had gotten her a corsage and a special birthday hat. She seemed to enjoy the attention, but yet I don't think she truly understood what the fuss was all about. This was Jim's first visit to see Mom. He was not at all comfortable about being there.

May 13, 2011

Today's visit was very emotional for me, as I realize that my Mom is slipping farther and farther away. There is nothing I can do to help her, other than to just be there and listen to her tell her stories, which seems to be enough for her. Mom was totally lost in her own world. While she talked to me, her stories were all about

World War II. She felt so sorry for all of those boys. They came to the back door looking for food and a place to hide and to be safe. She said that she took them down to the basement so they could hide. She gave them popcorn, soda, BBQ and ice cream. Mearl was one of the soldiers and so was Elvis. She said that Elvis was so grateful for her help, that he comes to visit her quite often.

May 23, 2011

Mom is part of a little group of ladies that I truly enjoy spending time with. They all laugh and tell such cute stories. I have learned a lot about these ladies. Some are happy go lucky, carefree spirits. A few must have been quite bossy and very opinionated in their day! Some, just sweet and lovely and wanting to be loved; others could care less about any of us. I asked one woman if she was a nun, she laughed out loud, and said, "From your lips to God's ears!" She looked up towards the ceiling; pointing her finger into the air, laughing and said, "Did you hear that?"

One sad, teary-eyed lady, just wants to go home; nothing or no one can make her happy.

I notice that the Move-In-Coordinator is walking a family around. She brings the family to the table where I am sitting and introduces me to the daughter. I know that look in her eyes. I had that same look and feelings myself just a few short weeks ago. I got up from my chair, so that her Mother could sit with the other ladies. As I moved off to the side, so did the daughter. We connected immediately. She leaned into me and said, "This is so hard." We turned so that her Mother would not see her crying. I hugged her and said, "Yes, I know, even though we know this is for the best, it does not make it any easier." The Move- In - Coordinator turned to me and said, "I was so glad to see you here today. I knew you would be good for each other."

(I often cry on my lonely drive back home after visiting with Mom. Today, I still cried, but it was different. Today, I felt I had served a purpose. I also realized that God does work in mysterious ways. I was there at that particular moment for a reason. Today, I had come full circle and could be of help to someone else. When I told that daughter that I understood how she felt, she knew that I really did. They were not just empty,

well-intended words. They were from a true common bond of the heart.)

MAY 2009
MOM'S 79TH BIRTHDAY
PARTY
LINDA, MOM, JIM, ME

12
PLASTIC PINWHEELS

January 2, 2012

It is a cold, very windy, gray afternoon. There isn't a single ray of sun shining through the bare winter branches. The wind is howling like we live in the North Pole. My dogs, Brodey and Harley, have decided that it is time to go outside. I put on my shoes and my jacket to go out with them. As we cross the threshold of the doorway, out of the corner of my right eye, I notice something moving. I look to see the two large, colorful, plastic pinwheels that are sitting in a lifeless, sleeping flower bed, spinning like crazy. Out of nowhere, I am instantly flooded with memories as my eyes fill with tears and a smile crosses my mouth at the same time.

In May of 2009, I threw Mom a semi-surprise 79th birthday party. Semi-surprise, because she knew we were planning a party, but she did not know that family and friends were coming from great distances to wish her a Happy Birthday. She thought it was just my brother and sister and her whole family. I had told her that we were having the party at the church hall, since I have a small house, there would be plenty of room for all the grandkids to run around and play outside on the playground. She thought that was a very good idea. She was thrilled with the idea that it was a party just for her, because she had never had a birthday party before. I also knew that time was running out in order for me to give her a party that she would remember, even if for just a little while.

It was a garden theme; food was served in new clean, plastic flower pots and plant saucers. Potted plants were table centerpieces and take home gifts for our guests. Brightly colored silk butterflies and hummingbirds hung from the ceiling, and outside there were several large plastic pinwheels marking which door of the church hall was the party entrance. After the party, Mom and I each took a couple of the pinwheels home for each of our flower beds. I did not know then how they would become a bond of what was yet to come.

In the weeks following the party, it kept becoming clearer to me how quickly Mom's memory was declining, and yet my siblings could not, or would not see it. This had me questioning once again my own judgment and wondering if I was making too much of her forgetfulness. Was it just normal aging?

I had already been doing a lot of research on dementia and Alzheimer's disease, but I knew that I needed to know more. I started seeking out lectures and support groups, desperately trying to figure what was "normal" and what would trigger the need for more care. Through listening to the stories of others; professionals, family members and patients themselves, I learned a lot of tips. I was made aware of what a fine line there is separating the normal aging and the "more", and some of the signs that I needed to be looking for. One of those signs is that if your loved one is telling a story and cannot think of the correct word and then either tries to act out the word or searches for a similar use. (e.g. trying to come up with the word watch, but instead points to their wrist and talks about that thing that tells the time, the clock you wear here on your arm, etc.).

One afternoon while visiting with Mom, we were talking about how windy it was outside. She said, "Yes, I have been sitting here watching that,... that......that," she raised her arm up in the air and made a circling motion and then a swooshing wind sound from her mouth. I knew that I was getting one of those signs that I could no longer doubt my own instincts, regardless of what my brother and sister chose to see or NOT see.

Today, the smile on my teary face comes from the memory from well over fifty years ago. A beautiful woman with thick, long, dark brown, naturally wavy hair and bright, blue eyes that sparkled as she taught her little girl, with the dark brown, Shirley Temple curls, how to blow on a small, plastic pinwheel; making the brightly colored spokes spin around and around, and not poke her eyes with the sharp points.

Thank you, Lord, for my own personal ray of sunshine on this gray day. One never knows what will spark a memory, just keep your eyes and your heart open and let the wind speak to you. HE knows what you need, and HE will provide. Those bright green, blue and yellow stripes will forever spin and weave together memories shared between a mother and her daughter. I know that I will never look at the spinning pinwheels the same way again. I will be reminded of my Mother every time the wind blows.

Though one cannot remember;
Another, hopes to never forget.

It had been an extremely hectic week, of meetings and appointments, with various doctors, lawyers, and several different support group meetings. I was exhausted, but I had one more support group meeting to go to on this particular evening. No time to eat dinner; I forced myself into the car, wishing I could take a nap on the couch instead. As I drove away from the house and headed towards the highway, I became overwhelmed with just how tired I was. I thought about the 20 mile drive to get to the meeting, and then there would be the 20 mile drive back home around 9:00 p.m. How tired would I be by that time? I decided that I just could not do it. I really had reached my limit. I turned around and drove back home. As I was reaching for the latch on the wooden gate into my yard, I heard some familiar words echo in my head, "Honey, you can't do it all!"

(My Mom had just given me permission to go take that nap on the couch and not feel guilty about it. I really need to learn to pace myself.)

Mom had rarely been to a beautician in her life. She was never one to make the weekly trip to get her hair "done." She had always relied on my sister to cut and perm her hair when needed. On the rare occasion that she did go, she was pleased with what they had done, but it was still out of her realm of normalcy.

During her time in assisted living and now in Memory Care, she learned to feel special when she got her hair done. However, in a dementia patient, things can change quite quickly and for no apparent reason.

I received a phone call saying that, "Miss Virginia, has hit the hairdresser. She can no longer have her hair done by our beautician." Knowing that the beautician is an outside person who comes in to provide this service, I completely understood her feelings, and knew she did not have to put up with being hit. So now it would be up to me to cut her hair as needed. I am a pretty crafty person, but I am not a hairdresser. I will do the best that I can, but I am afraid it will more likely appear that Mom cut her own hair when I am finished with it!

13

ONE YEAR LATER

It has been one year since Mom moved into the Memory Care Unit. It has been a year full of many changes, a lot of turmoil and confusion, but most importantly a lot of new discoveries, and many special memories.

I can remember March 14, 2011, like it was yesterday. I can still see the fear and the hate in Mom's eyes, as she realized that she was not going home with us. I can still hear her yelling at me about "dumping her somewhere" and to "just get the hell out of there." As much as it broke my heart to leave her there, I knew it was the best thing for her. I kept hoping and praying that I was doing the right thing.

A year later, it still breaks my heart that I have to see my Mom wilting away before my very eyes. I see her blue eyes turning gray and the sparkle is no longer there. I watch her body becoming more hunched over, and weaker. But these are physical things that are expected as we age.

It can be very devastating to watch a person's mind virtually disappear. I never know from one day to the next what kind of a mood she will be in when I arrive. I don't know what or who she will remember. She may be laughing and talking non-stop about nothing at all, singing little childhood songs, or she may be angry and downright mean, and nothing can make her happy.

The one thing that I have come to realize, is that being with Mom, is like being with a two year old. Yes, I have heard this and read it so many times over the past years, but for me now, it has become real.

Everyone knows the "terrible twos" of raising a child. They want to be independent and do everything for themselves. Yet, as the adult, we know they need help and guidance; sometimes the child will accept the help, more times than not.....they fight it....and yell, "*I CAN DO IT MYSELF*"!!

Mom's favorite response to everything is, "I AM 80 YEARS OLD, I CAN DO IT MYSELF"!!! "I will take a shower when I am ready!" *(She is never ready!)*

After eating a Mardi Gras cupcake that was heavily covered in bright yellow, green and purple frosting, and having frosting all over her hands and face, a CNA arrived with a wet wash cloth to clean up the sticky mess. Mom tosses her head back and forth, pulling her hands away from the aide, and yelling, "No! No! No!"

Once that moment was over, she was fine and telling me all about the party again.

Shower time has become such an ordeal. I have been a firsthand witness and assistant with the shower. I ended up as wet as she was! She screamed and fought it so badly, she sounded like a poor dying animal. Someone on the outside would have thought she was being beaten. I had brought in a tub of pink buttermints from Cracker Barrel and used them as bribes, something to divert her mind a bit. I asked if shower time is always this bad. The aide replied that this was nothing compared to what it is usually like. (*Poor girl has had a busted lip from trying to give Mom a shower and Mom has had bruises from putting up such fierce battles.*) Once Mom was dried off and dressed, she was fine and happy again. I kept telling her how pretty she was, and how good she smelled. But the ordeal of the shower has gotten so bad, that the doctor has now ordered a mild anti-anxiety pill to be given 30 minutes before each shower.

Potty training should be pretty well established by the age of two, but of course there are always the accidents! Now at 83, Mom has had to give up the regular ladies underwear for the adult diaper. Sadly, when she has an accident, she must be trying to clean it up herself and in the end is actually playing in it and causing a huge nasty mess, or she tries to hide it, like in a drawer or in her closet with clean clothes. Numerous books and cards and family pictures have had to be thrown away, because they were ruined. EEWWW!!

There is no rhyme or reason as to what goes on inside the mind of an Alzheimer's patient. One can only imagine how confused they must feel. One day can be a very good, happy go lucky day full of chatter and song. The next day, or sometimes even the very next minute, is filled with pure vile and angry words. There can be non-stop cursing (from a woman who would NEVER swear before).

Sometimes, she just lies in her bed and does not want to visit or socialize in any way. She lies there all curled up in a near fetal position. I sit in the chair and watch her rest. She opens her eyes and says, "you're still here, go on get-out-a- here," and then closes her eyes again. I watch a few more minutes and she opens her eyes again. This time her voice is a bit sharper as she states, "**get**", and again closes her eyes. So to minimize her stress, I kiss her forehead, tell her I love her, then turn to leave.

There are several things that I have learned through this past year. The most important thing is that I can never plan what a visit will be like, or what we will do. I must remain flexible and just go with the mood of the moment. I know she does not intend to be mean and ugly; it is just a horrible reality of this mind--stealing disease. I thank God that He has given me the strength to handle this task much better than I would have ever dreamed possible. While it is not easy to see Mom in this condition, I know that it is in some unknown reason…God's way. Maybe someday, it will make sense, but for now, we both try to make the best with the cards we were dealt.

The other lesson that I am learning, is the hardest one of all; dealing with people on the outside of the situation, the ones who are not a part of the day to day living among the Alzheimer world. For me, these people are divided into two categories. There are some who are unaware and do not want to be aware. They want to live their lives with no emotional connections to the situation at hand. Sadly, they are missing out on precious time and memories.

The second group are the ones who "know it all," even though they too are not living it, or are a connected part of it. They think they have all the answers and are not at all hesitant at saying what they feel that I should be doing, or how I should be handling a situation. They question my every move or thought, destroying every ounce of confidence that I have in myself and the situation...

There are hundreds of books and websites on living in and among the Alzheimer's world. However, no amount of reading and research can truly prepare a person for the reality of it. If you are not personally invested in the situation, you really have no idea of what the patient or the caregiver is thinking or feeling. Most people who are giving their unsolicited advice, are only saying what they think are the right words to say, the right words for them, or what they think I need to hear. I try to give them the benefit of the doubt. I know that they mean well and they think that they are helping. In reality, I know that they too are struggling through their own confusion of this disease, just as both Mom and I are struggling in our own ways.

Mom still tells her stories of Elvis and Mearl Justus being there to eat with her and what good visits that the three of them have. I have learned, she tells these stories to everyone. Since she is living in Madison county, not everyone that she talks to is even aware of who Mearl Justus is. I am always asked, "Who is this Mearl Justus that she talks about?" I tell them that he is her cousin, he is the St. Clair County Sheriff and she is quite proud of him and his accomplishments. Then a look of wonder comes across their faces. The next question is always, "Then Elvis is her cousin too?" It is an interesting concept, and oh, if it could only have been true! But that part of the story is in her fantasy world.

She also tries to use her family connection to the sheriff to her advantage when necessary, especially at shower time, or any other time that she does not want to do whatever the staff is asking of her. Whenever she wants to be stubborn, and prove that she is in control, she tells them, "I am calling the sheriff on you! He is my cousin, and he will make you stop!"

14

SHE'S A STUPID WOMAN

It was April 7, 2012. The Easter Bunny had just finished his visit to the Memory Care Unit. Mom was not overly excited about his presence. She smiled and thought he was cute; unlike like last year, when she spotted him coming down the hallway, and she jumped up and ran off towards him shouting, "Honey Bunny, it's the Honey Bunny, he's here." Then she proceeded to follow his every step. This year she did not get out of her chair or even care at all when he walked away after having his picture taken with her.

Following his visit there was some time yet before lunch was served. We did our usual walk around to look at pictures. Looking at our family picture taken 3 years ago for her 80th birthday, I asked who the people were. Pointing to herself, she proudly proclaimed, "This is me!" I asked who the other people were. Her first response was, this is Elvis, (pointing to my brother Jim), this is Elvis' girlfriend, (pointing to me) and this is his Mom, (pointing to my sister Linda). I kind of chuckled, and said, "No, this one is me". She looked at me, looked back at the picture and back at me again, and then she said, "No, I don't think so, you are prettier than this person in the picture." This made me smile.

Then we went to her personal story board outside her door. The story board is a frame filled with pictures and information just outside each resident's room, created by their family members. It helps the staff to know who the people were, before they were robbed of their memories. It gives them information for interacting with their charges. It helps the residents to remember who they were, as well.

Mom and I usually walk the complete tour of the hallway, looking at each and every story board. Her favorite ones are the ones who have pictures of little kids in them.

Mom is so very proud of her senior picture from Mercy High School. Right away, she was saying, "See me, that is me, Mercy High School, Mercy High School, Mercy High School." I pointed to her and Dad's wedding picture and asked who those people were. She said she did not know them. I told her that the pretty woman in the picture was her. A very angry and upset look came over her face, she said, "I do not know who that woman is, but I do know that she is very, very stupid. She is so stupid! I just want to kill her." After I caught my breath and got over the initial shock I asked, "Why would you want to kill her, she is a very pretty woman." She continued on with a very lengthy, mean and hateful monologue:

"That woman is so stupid. She just sits there and does not talk to him at all, and he just sits there and never talks to her either. She is so stupid, she should just leave. Just show him! But no-o-o-o, she just stays, she is so stupid! She asks him if they could just go for a ride in the car, just go somewhere, do something. The man says, "NO!" So she just sits and doesn't talk to him anymore, and he does not talk to her. She is so stupid."

. So I ask about the man, "But he really is a nice man, though, isn't he?" She replies, "**W- E- L- L!!,** he looks like he should be a nice man, but he isn't! He is clean, and dresses nicely, and most people think that he is nice, **BUT HE'S NOT!!!** He is so mean! He is not nice at all. He has everybody fooled! All she wants to do is go for a ride in the car, and he does not ever want to do anything that she wants to do. He is mean, and says, "NO" and then he won't talk to her anymore, and she just sits there and doesn't talk to him anymore either. How can a woman be so stupid? She should leave, but she is too stupid"

I redirected her thoughts to another picture on the story board, so that she would quit thinking about those days that made her so unhappy.

I have known my entire life that Mom and Dad did not have a happy marriage, that she stayed in the beginning because she did not have a way to support herself and her kids. In later years, she still held out hope that he would somehow change, that he would somehow become a compassionate person, but instead he got sick and she became his caretaker. But to hear her talk about the stupid woman, just broke my heart. It was so upsetting to hear that she thought so little of herself as a woman. Now with the dementia, she is able to verbalize feelings that had been suppressed for so many years. I am getting a glimpse of the woman that she wanted to be and couldn't. I wonder if this is why Richard plays such an important part of her current world. While I know their relationship was a whole lifetime ago and they were both so young at the time, they must have cared very deeply for each other. She must deeply long for, what I believe to be, the one true love of her life.

15

CAUTION . . . .

SHARP LEFT BANK AHEAD !!!!

I had seen this horrendous curve coming for almost three years and had hoped and prayed that somehow it could be avoided, but it is here and we are trying to hold on to what we can.

Back in 2009, when we were first preparing to get Mom moved into assisted living, I was also trying to prepare my brother for how all of this was going to change his life as well. I really thought he understood the impact of losing Mom's income as well as his "Mommy" who did EVERYTHING for him.

I tried to explain to him that when she moved into assisted living, that ALL of her income went with her. He would be totally on his own, to pay ALL of his own expenses, utilities and mortgage. I was met with cold blank stares as well as retorts of, "I am not stupid", and "I know that!"

As I tried to offer moral and emotional support and to be there for him without getting into his personal business, his male pride and inherited stubbornness always took over. He would tell me that he was handling things, he was okay, and that it was none of my business. I tried to convince myself that he was 40 something years old and that I was not his "Mommy" and if he was ever going to grow up, it would have to be the hard way. I could not do everything for him, as well as be the only person responsible for Mom's well-being. I pretty much left him alone, talked and checked up on him frequently, but stayed out of his business.

Jim is a very quiet, reserved person and rarely offered up any information on anything. Having a conversation with Jim is like pulling teeth. I ask questions, he responds with simple one word answers. He never asked questions nor sought opinions or advice; he has lived his life with his head in the sand, assuming that if he ignored the burdensome things in life, they would go away. He never learned how to tackle a problem head on. Mom would always rescue him from whatever problems came his way; she did all of his thinking for him. He never learned to figure it out for himself.

Unfortunately for him, about this same time, the girlfriend of several years decided that she needed some space and they should just be friends. From conversations that she and I had had; I am certain that she was afraid of him becoming totally dependent upon her and she did not want to become that involved or turn into his "Mommy figure."

Here we are, June 2012, the foreclosure notice was served a month ago, which he did not respond to or acknowledge. I know that the eviction notice is coming any day now. While there is nothing left in the house of any real monetary value, there are things that Jim will need, no matter where he goes to live, things such as dishes, towels and personal keepsakes. My dear husband, Dan has offered to set him up with a small storage unit, in order to get some of those necessary items out of the house before the doors are padlocked. I have suggested that he pack a suitcase of clothes to carry in the trunk of his car, so that he will have more than just the clothes on his back.

When I asked him why he let it get this far, why didn't he do something to prevent this situation from getting so out of hand, his reply was that he was scared and too stubborn to ask for help.

I know I have relied heavily on God's help during the last few years, and I know this ride is far from over, but I REALLY need a guiding hand through this curve! A large part of me wants to say, the house is not in Mom's name and he created this mess; why should I help bail him out? Of course I will help, because I am his sister and it is the right thing to do. But I really do not feel that I should be responsible for a 40-something-year-old man, and my kind and generous husband certainly should not be expected to come to his rescue. He needs to take some responsibility for himself.

As I walk down the hall towards Mom's room, I am looking at other residents rooms. Looking at the pictures, plants and other decorations sitting on their nightstands, wishing I could do the same for Mom. I am also thinking that many people look into Mom's room and must think that she has no one who cares. Her room is so sparse. (*Why do I worry about what other people think?*)

While many aspects of dementia are the same for everyone, it is also very different. Each person has their own uniqueness in what they can comprehend.

Most people do not know that I have brought in pictures; that Mom tore up and threw away. Framed pictures she has stashed away in her drawer. At each visit, I set the pictures out, we talk about them and who is in them. Mom promptly returns them back to the drawer.

For Mother's Day I took Mom a Kalanchoe Plant, at my next visit, I was checking the plant to see if it needed water. Mom reached over, picked off some of the tiny white flowers and promptly put it in her mouth, saying, "It is good." Like any mother does with her child, I stuck my finger in her mouth to retrieve the flowers before she could swallow them. Of course, she is trying to fight me off, while telling me that it is popcorn and that it is good. The plant went home with me that very day!

On another visit, I brought a vase of cut flowers. I took great care to make sure that it was a plastic vase, nothing that could be broken and cause harm. She thought it was very pretty. When I returned the next day, the flowers and the vase were gone. I looked around and found the vase of flowers lying in her underwear drawer. Yes, everything was wet. Cards, books and letters were ruined. When I asked her why she put them in the drawer, she said, "I don't like them."

Well meaning family members who are not fully aware of what Mom's world is like, bring big boxes of candy and snack cakes. Little do they realize that as soon as they leave, she will eat the whole thing without stopping! I have watched her grab both hands full of chocolate and shove it in her mouth, ending up with chocolate all over her, then fighting me during the clean-up process.

I feel like I should apologize to the people who left those two pound boxes of chocolates, because if I found it sitting there, half gone, I took it home. She had obviously had enough for the time being. If it will make you feel better, I sorted the remainder into little baggies and brought it back a few pieces at a time.

But, seriously, why do I think I owe you an apology, when you didn't ask if was okay to leave that much candy sitting around for her? Would you put a two pound box of chocolates in front of a two year old child and leave them alone with it? Did you ask me or the nursing staff if she was on any kind of restricted diet? Were you aware when she was put on a pureed foods, because she could no longer chew properly?

16

THE RIDE GOES ON

It is early June 2012 - we are having such a heat-wave already, that it feels like it should be late July or August. We have not had any rain in quite a while, so I am out very early this morning watering plants and shrubs. I don't mind this early morning peaceful chore in my yard. It gives me time to reflect on God's Blessings that He has given me during my life.

I am 60 years old. I have had my loving husband, Dan, by my side for 43 of those years. We have supported each other through some very rough and scary times, as well as, many loving and cherished moments. We have three healthy, beautiful daughters, three handsome sons-in-law and two wonderful grandsons. We have had no serious illnesses or injuries. My husband works very hard at a job that allows me the privilege to stay at home and run our small home-based ceramic business, as well as to be "on-call" for any of Mom's needs. We live an average middle-class lifestyle. We are not rich in material things or money by any means. I know that we have more than many other people have, and yet, not as much as others. We live in a small house in an unincorporated area of the county. We bought this house very quickly because it answered so many of our needs at the time. Is it the perfect dream home? Not at all, but it is "home." I thank God for providing what was needed, and allowing me to be here to watch over my Mom.

My Mother's life when she was 60, had known lots of heartache and deep loss. She grew up in Chicago, during the depression and had very little in the way of extras. She had lost a very dear brother in a car accident when he was just 18 years old. Her Dad had died of prostate and colon cancer. She herself had severe stomach problems and had more than half of her stomach removed. In 1976, she lost her oldest son Bob, (who had been named for her deceased brother) in a tragic car accident, also just 18 years old. In 1989 when Mom turned 60, she was working full time at Bridal Originals, coming home to be my Dad's full time caretaker, as well as transporting him to and from kidney dialysis three times a week; never relinquishing any of her household duties of shopping, cooking and cleaning, and never complaining, either.

Did the stresses of her life contribute to her dementia? Will my easier life protect me? Who knows? We don't have those answers yet.

What I do know, is that God provided the means, and the home, for me to be where I needed to be at this time in our lives. I am very grateful for the life He has given me. I intend to do the job that he has put before me to the very best of my abilities.

June 26, 2012

For now, I believe that the worst is behind me; the scariest twists and turns have been handled and we are riding along pretty smoothly. While there is an occasional dip here and there, I have come to realize that I can handle whatever comes next. I am actually stronger than I ever thought I could be. I have grown in what I have learned; I realize that I am not alone with my fears and insecurities. I know that the most important thing is that Mom is in a safe and secure place. She is in generally good health, she herself is calm and at peace with herself and her surroundings. I have done everything in my power to insure her health and safety. I now have to trust God's Will, and His Mercy. He is in control, and I trust that He will be by my side in that roller coaster car whenever we go again with the elevated twists and turns.

I'm sorry to say, that I know my brother is struggling with hanging on to the house that he cannot afford to keep. Yet will not make an effort to get rid of it, nor even discuss with me what his options might be. He won't ask for help and will not accept any advice. I can't help him, if he doesn't want any help. The foreclosure papers have been served, yet he is still in denial of what is to come.

Today at my annual physical, my doctor's advice was that it is now time to put me first. It is time to take care of my own health. Of course, the prescription is: "Diet, Exercise, and Rest." He told me I was worth it, and you know what, he **is** right. **I am worth it!!**

While my Mom will always be the top priority in my life, starting today.......

I intend to start taking care of me!
Until the next big curve; and of course we know, without a doubt, there will be one!

July, 2012
Mom had been served with foreclosure papers at the nursing home on the same day that Jim had been served. I followed the instructions and went to the courthouse to give an answer to the courts. When I explained that the

bank that was pursuing the foreclosure was actually the second mortgage holder, that Mom was in a nursing home with the assistance of state aid, and that the first mortgage was in my brother's name only. They told me to go home, that I had nothing to be concerned about.

I had a nagging feeling that there had to be more to this, that something just wasn't right with the whole thing. I also knew that calling my attorney would probably be of no use. I'm sure this would not be in his scope of law. I did an internet search on Elder Law, found a female lawyer, and made an appointment. *(Frankly, I had grown tired of men's excuses and lack of interest and concern.)*

I presented all the information that I had accumulated over the last several years to the attorney and her assistant. Within 15 minutes I learned that in 2003 when Mom and Jim had transferred the house into his name only, they did not complete the process. They had refinanced the loan, but did not file a new deed at the courthouse. The house is still in her name, as well as his. It is jointly owned. Now, it is my problem too!

If I had known this important fact 3 years ago, things would have been handled so differently during these last months and years. But this chapter of the story, deserves an entire book of its own, and will be detailed at a later date.

I am notified that the life insurance policy that I had inquired about a couple of years ago, has been sold and I can now surrender the policy for cash. I contact the state of Illinois to let them know about the latest discovery. I am given the option to take Mom off of aid and do a private pay with the insurance money until which time she could be reinstated, or I can send the state a check for the full amount received as payment towards what they have already paid for Mom's care.

In light of the current affairs of the state, I did not want to risk taking her off of aid and then for some reason or other, she would not be reinstated. I told them I would mail them a check for the amount received along with documentation showing the policy had been sold.

The state was also entitled to half of the profit from the sale of the house. They were entitled to half, because the house was jointly owned with my brother; he was entitled to keep half. After many months of hard work by a very dedicated real estate agent, we avoided foreclosure and managed to sell the house, but there was no profit. In fact, my heaven-sent agent, wrote a personal check at the closing in order to pay the difference to close the sale. God truly took care of this situation for me.

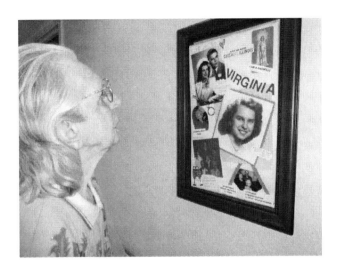

APRIL 2012

LOOKING AT HER STORYBOARD – TALKING ABOUT THE STUPID WOMAN

17

CONCLUSION

November, 2012

Our ride is not over, but it is time for me to put an end to the telling of this story. It is time for this part of our ride to be shared with others.

I feel I have written enough to give others an insight into our struggles with Alzheimer's. While the disease is very different for everyone involved, there are many similarities as well. I have shared the times when Mom's moods were downright mean and nasty to everyone around her. I hope I have also conveyed her fear and confusion, that I know she must have felt and could not verbally express. I hope too, that I have shown that there can be joy and hope. There have been many days where we shared smiles and laughs and song that I will treasure always. These last few years have been years of special memories that I am so grateful that I was able to share with my Mom.

More than anything else, I hope that others who may find themselves in the role of a caretaker, will see that they are not alone. While we are sharing this

Alzheimer's ride with our loved ones, we are also on our own roller coaster ride of emotions, fears, and self-doubts, as well as hope, love, and pride that we are doing the best job that we can.

I see that our ride on this roller coaster is slowing down and we are calmly coasting towards the end now; (I think!)

Mom quit walking in October, and as of Thanksgiving week, she quit eating on her own. The CNAs now play the "baby" games of feeding her, one talking and getting her to laugh while another CNA slips a spoon full of food in her mouth. But after a few bites, she is still smart enough to know that she is not in control. So, she quits laughing and talking and will not open her mouth to take a bite. The CNAs switch places and the game is on again.

Mom no longer has the strength to do real physical battle in the shower, though she does still try to fight; she likes to yell, "You're killing me! I'm 80 years old, I can do it myself!" She has yelled that from the first time they gave her a shower and I am sure she will say it when they give her last shower as well.

I know our time on this ride is getting shorter, and one day, she will be called home where she belongs. I hope that somewhere deep inside, she knew that I was

CONCLUSION

there for her and with her. I hope I was the one who put those beautiful smiles on her face, even though we were both very scared.

Following months of legal battles and countless phone calls between banks, lawyers, and realtors, we avoided foreclosure and the house was sold. The remnants of her life, packed in boxes and tubs, still scattered in every corner of my home, garage and basement, waiting for me to purge through it all. Mom's health declined and hospice was called in. The stress of it all took its toll on my own health and knocked me down and nearly helpless for several months. But by the grace of God, I was given my strength back, in order to continue on with the ride He has put us on.

The ride continues on.........

........together.........

......as long as it lasts........

Senior Prom
Mercy High School—class of 1948
Virginia Mae Wayne—second from left
her date, Richard, standing behind her

My brother Jim declined my offer for him to include his own thoughts, feelings or opinions to this story.

18

A LETTER FROM LINDA

"MY MOM, THE ALZHEIMER VICTIM"

The best way I know to start is from the beginning. From what I have read and heard, my Mom had a rough childhood. She was born in the depression and they didn't have much money. Her family had to keep moving to find a way of living, changing her from one school to another. Once she was able to get settled in and make friends, it seems they would have to move again.

The years in her life when I was a child were not a whole lot better for her. We didn't have to move around, we lived in the same house our whole lives growing up, but we never really had very much money. Mom did everything around the house until us kids were old enough to lend a helping hand. She had her hands full with Carolyn, me, Bob and Jim.

We never really went anywhere, Dad didn't want to. All he would want to do was watch the television while Mom would have to keep all of us tended to and quiet.

Mom was finally able to get a job when we were older, but life still wasn't peaches 'n cream. We only had one car, so she had to get a ride to and from work from someone else. If she was just a few minutes late, which wasn't her fault, Dad would be mad. Carolyn and I always had to get supper cooked every night, right after school since Dad liked to have supper on the table as soon as he got home from work.

Carolyn and I were married when Dad got sick. Mom took care of him the best that she could. Always taking him to the doctor, hospital, and to kidney dialysis three times a week and still worked her full time job. Dad passed on May 30, 1993.

Mom worked as a seamstress, making dresses for many years. She also made doll clothes, crocheted and quilted. She had a busy life, but she would always be there for us whenever we needed her. I could either go to her house or call her on the phone. She would talk for a while and calm me down. She would always tell me, things will get better."

I don't know if your previous years in life have anything to do with Alzheimer's disease, but I'll bet the stress sure does not help.

Once a person retires from their daily work routine, it seems to me, that Alzheimer's retires your brain. Mom would go to the grocery store and forget where she parked. She had a car accident and did not remember having it. She left the stove on. The list goes on and on because she didn't really know that she was doing these things.

A couple of years ago, Mom came to stay a few days with us. I noticed that she hadn't changed her clothes while she was there. So I sneaked a peak in her bag, and she didn't even bring any clothes with her except for underwear. She didn't know. My daughter, Julie, and Mom were going to make brownies. Julie had to show her how to grease the pan. She did not remember how.

I have not been around Mom as much as I should, and I don't know a lot about Alzheimer's Disease, but she doesn't know who I am any more. There are not enough words to express my love for my Mom, Virginia.

Alzheimer's hurts everyone involved, not just the person that has it. I think it hurts the others even more than the person who has the disease.

I also send my Blessings to my sister, Carolyn, for all she has done to care for Mom. I only wish I could be nearer to help, but I can't. God Bless you, Carolyn, I love you!

Mom, I love you. I know I can't tell you things will get better like you used to tell me, but maybe someone else in the future can get better.

I Love You Mom!!!

Love,

Linda

19

AN OPEN LETTER:

"TO MY DAUGHTERS"

Dear Tina, Lisa, and Danielle,

As I have traveled on this journey with your Grandma, the three of you have been very much on my mind. Naturally, my concern has been that hopefully you will not have to go through this too. Aging is a process that hopefully, and God willing, we will all go through, and that is a good thing. Yes, we all want to look and act young forever, no one wants to really admit how old they are, but age is just a number, it is what we do and how we act that determines our "real" age.

Every gray hair and every wrinkle and line on my face represents the passing of time that was shared with each of you, creating memories that will last a lifetime, my lifetime, and more importantly, yours. Wonderful years spent raising three adorable little girls into strong, beautiful women.

Every aging parent says that they do not want to be a burden to their children. They do not want to live with them and invade their personal space. They also say, "Promise you will not put me in a nursing home." I heard those words from my Grandma Wayne, your Grandma Mers, and also my Mom, your Grandma Manring. I hope that God will allow me to live long enough to be able to say those same things to you!

Seriously, no one ever wants to admit that they need the help of skilled care, but to not recognize that the time has come to require such assistance does create a burden for your family. I hope that you will be understanding when I say, "Do not put me in a nursing home", but keep in mind that you will know, better than I will, when the time has come, and you need to do what is right. Not just for yourself, but also for me.

You will want to be noble and think that you can take care of me yourself. After all, that is what a loving daughter wants to do, to take care of the woman (and father) who gave her life. You will want to return the nurturing that you once received. None of the decisions that you will ever have to make will be harder than how to handle an aging parent. Let God be your guide, and listen with your heart: I love you and I trust that you will do what will be right for all of us. I pray more than anything that none of you will have to carry the burden alone, that you will be able to share with each other in that chapter of life. You MUST keep the lines of communication open between all of you and work together!! Discuss observations and concerns.

If for no other reason, do this, "Because, I'm the Mom and I said so!"

Love you more than you know,

Mom

"Honey, you can't do it all"

Virginia Manring